BEYOND ECONOMICS AND ECOLOGY:

The Radical Thought
of Ivan Illich

Ivan Illich

BEYOND ECONOMICS AND ECOLOGY:
The Radical Thought of Ivan Illich

Preface by
Jerry Brown
Governor of California

Edited and introduced by
Sajay Samuel

MARION BOYARS
London · New York

Published in The United Kingdom and the United States in 2013
by Marion Boyars Publishers
26 Parke Road
London SW13 9NG
www.marionboyars.co.uk

British Library Cataloguing in Publication Data is available
from the British Library.
A CIP catalog record for this book is available
from the Library of Congress.

ISBN: 978-0-7145-3158-8 (13-digit) print
ISBN: 978-0-7145-2360-6 (13-digit) e-book

Printed in England

CONTENTS

PREFACE

by Jerry Brown

IVAN ILLICH is not your standard intellectual. His home was not in the academy and his work forms no part of an approved curriculum. He issued no manifestos and his utterly original writings both confound and clarify as they examine one modern assumption after another. He is radical in the most fundamental sense of that word and therefore not welcome on any usual reading list. The authoritative *New York Review of Books* last mentioned him thirty years ago, one editor terming him too catastrophic in his thinking. The *New York Times*, in its 2002 obituary, dismissed his ideas as "watered-down Marxism" and "anarchist panache". Even in death, he deeply upset the acolytes of modernity.

I knew Ivan Illich and had the pleasure of enjoying many hours at his table in lively conversation with his friends in Cuernavaca, Oakland, State College, and Bremen. His gaze was piercing yet it was warm and totally embracing. His hospitality was unmatched and his aliveness and friendship well embodied his ideas that in print were so provocative – and difficult.

Illich was a radical because he went to the root of things. He questioned the very premises of modern life and traced its many institutional excesses to developments in the early and Medieval Church. In his writings, he strove to open up cracks in the certitudes of our modern worldview. He questioned speed, schools, hospitals, technology, economic growth and unlimited energy – even if derived from the wind or the sun. Yet, he flew constantly across continents and mastered rudimentary programming. He once told me computers were an abomination but many years later used them like a pro. Yes, there were contradictions and as you read these essays, take a step back. Probe for the deeper meaning.

As California's governor, I am building America's first high speed rail system and pushing a relentless expansion of renewable energy. Yet, I still reflect on Illich's ideas about acceleration and transportation and even energy. Illich makes you think. He forces you to question your own deepest assumptions. And as you do, you become a better thinker.

Illich said equity would not come with more economic growth. That's a hard doctrine. We all want our GDP to grow. Yet look at the growth in inequality these last twenty years. Could he have seen that coming? Illich warned of counter-productivity, the negative consequences of exceeding certain thresholds. Are there tipping points in standardized schooling, medical interventions, transportation, energy consumption and the devices it makes possible? Illich wrote of learning as opposed to being taught in classrooms. Now the internet is opening access to knowledge and making learning possible outside of institutional constraints.

Illich early on warned of the ecological dangers of poisons and pollution generated by modern technologies, but he thought the breakdown in our social and cultural traditions was more pressing and more dangerous.

The way he lived, the simplicity and the caring of one human being for another, illuminates the underlying message of all his writings. He saw in modern life and its pervasive dependence on commodities and the services of professionals a threat to what it is to be human. He cut through the illusions and allurements to better ground us in what it means to be alive. He was joyful but he didn't turn his gaze from human suffering. He lived and wrote in the fullness of life and confronted – with humor and uncommon clarity – the paradoxes and contradictions, the possibilities and yes, the limitations of being mortal.

These essays will provoke you but they will also shine some light on the wonders of our time, its dangers and accompanying illusions.

Jerry Brown
Governor of California
May 2013

AFTER ILLICH:
an Introduction

by Sajay Samuel

THE ECOLOGICAL and economic crises have passed. The word 'crisis' derives from the Greek *krisis*, which referred to that moment in the course of an illness when it decisively turns towards either health, as when a fever breaks into a sweat, or death, as when the pulse fatally weakens. Crisis marks the moment beyond the fork in the road, when the road not taken fades into the distance.

The economic crisis is behind us because 'full employment' is no longer thought to be achievable, whether in advanced or emerging economies. Billions worldwide are unemployed. Millions more are underemployed or belong to the class of the "working poor" whose wages do little to lift them from misery. The ecological crisis is in the past as well in that the physical environment surrounding humans has turned inhospitable to many. Disappeared forests, privatized lands, paved streets, and foul airs are but some of the features of degraded land on which few can subsist.

Even as they dimly recognize it, many react to this state of affairs with a mix of resistance, anger, and fear. From Puerta del Sol in Madrid to Zuccotti Park in New York City, young and old have agitated for work. Hundreds of thousands eagerly seek low wages jobs available only to a tiny fraction. Desperate to obtain employment, many students borrow money to pay for the privilege of working as interns. On Earth Day 2012, although millions of people assembled from Melbourne to Maui to protest intensifying environmental degradation, research funds now pile up for geo-engineering on a planetary scale. Proposed schemes include stirring the oceans to absorb more carbon, as if seawater were simply tea in a giant cup. In towns and counties across central Pennsylvania, citizens accept poisoned aquifers and waterways as necessary consequences of "clean" natural gas.

Forty years ago, Ivan Illich (1926-2002) foresaw the coming crises. He argued that the industrialized societies of the mid-twentieth century, including communist Russia and capitalist USA, were already burdened by too much employment and too much energy. Explaining that habituation to employment frustrates and destroys self-reliance, and that the increasing power of machines deepens dependence on them, Illich warned against those whose misunderstanding of 'crisis' would perversely bring on what they sought to avoid. Even though this is precisely what they have wrought, politicians and scientists continue to stubbornly insist that the 'economic crisis' is simply a matter of not enough jobs and that the 'ecological crisis' is a matter of not enough clean energy. 'Not enough jobs' channels attention to creating more employment by expanding the economy, just as 'not enough clean energy' confines debate to getting more of it through techniques that reduce carbon emissions. This persistent fixation on more employment and more energy has now found expression in dreams of a so-called 'green economy', which in one stroke will somehow wipe out unemployment and renew the environment. It's a fixation that blinds us, Illich noted decades ago, to recognizing the thresholds beyond which useless humans will be forced to occupy uninhabitable environments.

Doubtless, the fear and anxiety of a jobless life is palpable to the intern who must pay to work in a job. So are the incomprehension and anger of the family who is homeless when displaced by a hurricane. But millions of others, who may be luckier, feel trapped between the pincers of shrinking paychecks and the rising costs of gas, heating oil, and food. For the many who must bear it, however, this feeling of vulnerability and precariousness need not lead to paralyzing despair. Instead, forced by their circumstances to acknowledge that widespread unemployment and a ravaged environment are here to stay, they may, with wisdom and humor, rediscover ways of living well. Precisely because good jobs and clean energy are now thought scarce, it is more than ever possible to begin the task of rethinking our attachments to 'employment' and 'energy'.

Selected from Illich's many essays, pamphlets and drafts, the four items reprinted here remain vitally important to that task.

Though written between 1973 and 1983, they retain an urgent relevance to those who must inhabit a world without secure employment or supportive environments. 'Employment is good', 'economic growth is necessary', 'technical innovations liberate', – these were unquestioned assumptions when Illich was writing these essays. They continue to maintain their grip on the collective imagination, although less tightly. Critical reconsideration becomes all the more difficult when an assumption has been left unquestioned long enough to be taken for a certainty and to even congeal into perception. Unlike many of his time and later, Illich's thought is radical in the sense of going to the roots of modern perceptions. These unsettling and disturbing pages are therefore likely to be useful now to those who seek to find a way, for whatever reason, beyond economics and ecology.

But the reader must exercise forbearance. First, these essays carry the mark of the confrontations Illich engaged in at the time. During the late 1960s through the early 1980s, Illich spoke to packed houses from San Francisco to Sri Lanka, was feted by politicians such as Indira Gandhi and Pierre Trudeau, engaged intellectually with the likes of Michel Foucault and Erich Fromm, and became a fierce and outspoken, if still obedient critic of the Roman Catholic Church which had once viewed him as a favorite son. Second, his thinking cannot be filtered through the political categories of left/right or progressive/conservative. They are unhelpful to fully appreciate a thinker who critiques both the market economy and the welfare state, who takes issue with the economic presuppositions held by both capitalist and socialist regimes, and who questions the supposed virtues of both 'family values' and working women. Third, and perhaps most important, his texts seem easy to read because he wore his considerable learning lightly. Their smooth surfaces belie finely wrought conceptual distinctions that support densely packed arguments. If they are to fully enjoy these sometimes polemical, sometimes humorous, but always sparingly crafted pieces of prose, readers who think they have read a text on skimming it will have to slow down and savor Illich's words.

Each of the four essays reprinted here was written for a specific occasion and together comprise only the smallest selection from a larger corpus questioning commodity and energy-intensive economies. The essays are presented thematically instead of chronologically to offer a better view of the sweep of Illich's argument. In the first two, *War against Subsistence* and *Shadow Work*, Illich reveals both the ruins on which the economy is built and the blindness of economics which cannot but fail to see it. The second two essays, *Energy and Equity* and *The Social Construction of Energy*, unearth the nineteenth century invention and subsequent consequences of 'energy' thought of as the unseen cause of all 'work' whether done by steam engines, humans, or trees. The science of ecology relies on this assumption and, as Illich explained, unwittingly fuels the addiction to energy. The close dance of energy consumption and economic growth is characteristic of not just industrially geared societies. After all, energy consumption steadily increases even in so-called post-industrial societies, fueling the fortunes of Google and Apple no less than Wal-Mart.

Historians have marked the transition from agrarian to industrial society by that phenomenon called the enclosure of the commons, seen vividly in Great Britain but elsewhere as well. The commons referred to the fields, fens, wastelands and woods to which access was free to all for pasturing livestock, planting crops, foraging for fuel wood, and gleaning leftover grain. Well into the eighteenth century, commoners comprised a substantial proportion of the British population and derived the greater portion of their sustenance from the commons instead of the market. From the mid-seventeenth century, but particularly over the hundred years until 1850, thousands of Enclosure Acts legalized enclosures that forced commoners to become landless peasants with no independent means of subsistence. Now fully dependent on paid work, they became the working class.

Privatizing the commons meant transforming land that was open to general use into an economic resource. Since scarce resources require legal and police protections, Illich insisted on not confusing the commons with public property. The latter no less than private property, is protected by the police, as for example are public parks and 'free speech zones'. In contrast, mutual aid, custom and customary rights among kin and interdependent households characterized use of the commons. The life in common was not devoid of market relations, as for example when working occasionally or purchasing salt. But as Illich noted in his essay *Useful Unemployment and its Professional Enemies*, "all through history, the best measure for bad times was the percentage of food eaten that had to be purchased." Commoning gave those who relied on it a floor against destitution. It is the vital importance given to provisioning over profiteering that accounts for such common customs as limits to the hoarding of grains during times of dearth. As the historians E.P Thompson and J.M. Neeson have explained at length, a moral economy encases and fetters the market economy when dependence on the market is balanced by the independence of self-subsistence.

However, Illich argued, the enclosure of the commons was but one chapter in a longer history of the war against subsistence. Indeed, it may not even be industrial products that best exemplify the separation of people from their ability to subsist. Instead, he suggested, 'the service economy' offers a more prototypical example for the separation of what economists call 'production' from 'consumption'. As Illich argued in *Vernacular Values*, in the same year that Columbus accidentally discovered the New World, Elio Antonio de Nebrija petitioned Queen Isabella of Spain to adopt "a tool to colonize the language spoken by her own subjects ..." From Catalonia to Andalusia, the Iberian peninsula of the fifteenth century was home to a profusion of vernaculars forged in the kiln of everyday trade, prayer and love. Columbus, who spoke several languages and wrote in a couple more that he could not speak, is a perfect example of how adept people can be without taught language skills. But Nebrija intended his Castilian grammar book and accompanying dictionary as tools to separate people from their untutored ability to speak. He intended for taught standardized language to discipline peoples' tongues in the interest of imperial power.

What was for Nebrija a stratagem of empire has by now become a need. In contemporary India, everyday speech is taught speech, whether it is the Hindi spoken at the store, the Tamil chattered at home, or the Boston English used to answer 1-800 help lines on behalf of Citibank. Speech is no longer uttered in the course of daily life but results from the consumption of a scarce commodity acquired from language instructors. For Illich, it is the modern professions that function as the most potent propagandists of human needs, whether for schools or for hospitals. Indeed, in his essay on the *Disabling Professions*, he argued that the construction of humans as needy beings was one of the most pernicious consequences of economic society. In the guise of experts, professionals discriminate against people by imputing a lack, an inability, or a need. They then mask such discrimination by justifying it as doing a service, prompted by their care. This expertly managed belief that humans are beings in need of services from certified professionals has deep roots beginning in the eighth century. As Illich elaborated in *Taught Mother Tongue*, it was then that priests became pastors by defining their "own services as needs of human nature" and by linking salvation to the obligatory consumption of those services.

Illich proposed to resuscitate the word "vernacular" in its historical reference to what is "homemade, homegrown and homebred", as a more fitting term than "subsistence", "human economies", or "informal sectors", to refer to what people do for themselves, whether that is singing, cultivating crops, building homes or playing. In the sense he gives the word, the vernacular denotes non-market activities, those not captured by the logic of exchange, without thereby implying a "privatized activity ... a hobby or an irrational and primitive procedure".

The separation of people from vernacular practices delivers them to a regime of scarcity. A dependence on scarce goods and services can be maintained by force, as with zoning laws prohibiting backyard or rooftop chicken coops. Compulsory schooling, like most other expert and professionally defined services, commands dependence by imputing legally sanctioned needs. But institutionalizing envy can also propel dependence on commodities. As Illich argued in *Gender*, traditional cultures recognized invidious comparison as destructive of social relations and devised symbolic forms such as the 'evil eye' to suppress it. But modern economies are organized to mask envy as a way to better disseminate it. 'Keeping up with the Joneses' or 'bettering one's condition' are slogans that rhetorically blunt what the pastor Bernard Mandeville in 1714 baldly stated as the formula for economic growth: private vices, public benefits.

Despite the contrary assertion of standard economics textbooks, Illich thus argues that modern economies do not solve the problem of scarcity. Instead, the economy is better understood as a machine for the production of scarcity, whether through force, need, or envy. The destruction of the vernacular is both cause and consequence of the economy, and, the resulting subject of the economy is possessive, invidious and needy. Economic ideologists of all stripes, including socialists and capitalists, are convinced of a human need for education and electricity. Their shared conviction reveals them as agents united in the ongoing war against the vernacular, advertised as the virtuous and uplifting cycle of work and consumption.

Throughout the Middle Ages, wage labor was considered a mark of the miserable and thought to be a fate worse than beggary. By the sixteenth century, labor was ennobled and dignified as work by the likes of Martin Luther and John Calvin. By the seventeenth century, those who stood to profit from it argued that work was a natural cure for poverty, which was seen as being caused by laziness or indolence. Conveniently, the assumption-turned-perception of work as natural overlooks that it is the very dependence on wages that modernizes poverty. As Illich pointed out, the modernized poor are those who are prevented from living outside the economy and yet are forced to occupy its bottom rungs.

But, argued Illich, the thoroughgoing dependence on cash is only the visible tip of an even deeper injustice. A society organized around putting people to work will necessarily create "shadow work", which Illich defined as the unpaid toil needed to make commodities and services fully useful. If one has to buy eggs because one cannot keep chickens, then the effort of going to the market, finding a parking spot, and returning home comprises frustrating shadow work. One is engaged in shadow work when doing one's homework because one is compelled to attend school, or when surfing the internet to get information on one's medical options. The hours lost in commuting to make oneself useful to an employer is shadow work necessary to "make a living".

Illich found the paradigm of shadow work in housework. Unlike commoners, workers in the modern economy typically do not consume directly the fruits of their labor. Until the early nineteenth century this forced separation of production from consumption fueled protracted protests, many led by women. Illich argued that these protests were quelled, in part, by glorifying the confinement of women to their houses. "The fairer sex" rhetorically ennobled the enclosure of women as housewives whose unpaid toil exemplifies the historically new sphere of shadow work. The house as the site of unpaid reproduction is the necessary shadow cast by the workplace as the space of paid production. The creation of unpaid work as a requirement that other work be paid, suggested to Illich that the subject of economics was also genderless. The economy is fundamentally sexist, he argued, because it recognizes the human only in its capacity to produce and reproduce. Even if women are drawn into the workforce and men are encouraged to help with childrearing, most of the unpaid toil is overwhelmingly borne by women. More generally, he speculated that the economy would collapse if all the shadow work required for its functioning were to be paid for. How much would Facebook be worth if its users were paid for their efforts to produce content and consume advertisements?

Shadow work remains hidden partly because it is sentimentalized. The defense of "family values" sentimentalizes sexist oppression by maintaining the fantasy that the modern house continues immemorial tradition, whereas the demand that housework be paid only exposes the paradoxical freedom sought in dependence on wage-work. Shadow work does not foster vernacular modes of living nor does it nourish the realm of autonomous being-together. Instead, it supports and deepens the dependence on a life given to employment, even when there are fewer jobs available. Parents devote countless hours to their children's homework to 'upgrade the human capital' that schooling delivers to the workplace. Illich noted that sentimentalizing such shadow work as 'quality time' is the kind of dishonesty needed to live with the iniquities inherent in commodity-intensive markets.

Forty years ago, Illich suggested self-service would be the species of shadow work that would likely expand faster than wage labor. That may have come to pass, when computer-prompted busywork such as online banking and deleting spam is added to the time spent on home improvement projects, life-long learning and unpaid internships. He also argued, in *Energy and Equity* that the continued growth of energy-intensive social arrangements would destroy more than just the physical habitat of men and women. In hindsight, his tightly argued warning and plea point to the road not taken as the crises gathered. It may however still offer hope to those now caught in the vise of endemic underemployment and a ravaged environment.

The widespread belief that economic growth comes at the cost of ecological despoliation overlooks the more decisive and prior destruction of the socio-cultural milieu of a people; the vernacular. For this reason Illich wrote in *Silence is a Commons* that the most virulent kind of ecological degradation occurs with "the transformation of the environment from a commons to a productive resource." It is not just that land then becomes real estate, viewed from a distance rather than trodden underfoot. Rather, economic values proliferate by engulfing the variegated ways of living in common, a kind of destruction reflected sharply in the steady vanishing of languages. While waste and pollution caused by economic growth describe environmental degradation, Illich recommended the term "disvalue" to name the denigration and destruction of the social environments necessary to propel that growth.

Not so long ago, services and commodities swirled only around the margins of everyday life. Today they are everywhere. For most of human history, tools were shaped to the natural abilities of their users. Today people function as appendages of their tools, which set the rhythm and pace of their lives. Whether they are cars or high-tech hospitals, when the quantity of commodities and services exceed a certain threshold of intensity, they exclude non-market alternatives and therefore impose what Illich called a radical monopoly.

Paved streets for cars and rails for trains demand the Earth be reshaped to fit.

But to this environment degradation must be added three kinds of frustration that results from the radical monopoly of energy-intensive commodities. Too many cars on the road spark 'road rage,' and too much education produces incurious teens. Both are examples of a frustrating subversion that Illich named technical counterproductivity. Speedy cars push bicycles and pedestrians off the streets just as too many emails and television shows overwhelm face-to-face conversations. This displacement of vernacular activity by economic artifacts he called structural counterproductivity. Just as consumers of too many passenger-miles believe they can move only when they are sitting on a moving seat, so the buyers of too many student credits believe they can learn only what they are taught. The self-perception of both expresses the cultural counterproductivity that result from the repeated use of packaged goods, just as myths are engendered by ritualized behaviors. That the ecological and economic problems are still understood in terms of scarcity, whether of clean energy or well-paid jobs, reveals how deeply self-perception has been shaped by the overuse and suffocating presence of commodity intensive markets and energy intensive technologies.

Economics and ecology cannot comprehend the vernacular, Illich argues in the *Social Construction of Energy*, because they mystify a social construction as a natural phenomenon. From its very beginnings, the science of ecology imbibed the assumption of scarcity and imputed it to the whole of nature. Bees and trees, whales and bacteria – all species are seen as locked in a battle over scarce nutrients. In documenting the twists and turns that scientists took during the nineteenth century to construct "energy" as the invisible and indestructible source of all "work", Illich shows how both work and energy, when used in everyday language, makes a scientific construction appear to be a natural phenomena. Whether aggregated as population or proletariat, individuals are understood en masse as a source of labor power to be worked. In the same timeframe, the universe or Nature itself came to be understood economically as an energy generator with the potential for work. Illich suggests the entwined assumptions that nature works and that work is a natural masquerade for certainties that now prop up a world built for energy-intensive employment.

To Illich, the differences between economics and ecology were less significant than the presumptions they shared. The economist wants to replace people with cheaper, more efficient machines. The ecologist wants to get rid of cars and replace them with energy saving bicycles. However, neither suspects that machines and people are incomparable, except as objects of science. For the scientist, "work" is done and "energy" is consumed by a steam engine, a rat, a data center and a pedestrian. And as ecologists and economists now form an alliance to tout the so-called "green economy", they subject the economy of commodities to the greater economy of energy. They tighten the noose of scarce resources without contributing to freedom from dependence on jobs and joules. As Illich noted many years ago, "radical monopoly would accompany high-speed traffic even if motors were powered by sunshine and vehicles spun of air."

The radical monopolization of vernacular life has now made it almost impossible to live without high-energy inputs, outside the cycle of work and consumption, beyond the grip of scarcity. Yet by the force of circumstance, this is the situation that many must now contend with as wage work dries up and shadow work grows. To protect the means of provisioning for themselves, commoners once agitated not for minimum wages but for a ceiling on the profits derived from enclosing the commons. They did not want a handout but instead insisted on the liberty to fend for themselves. Similarly, Illich argues that the speed of motor-powered vehicles on common streets be limited so as not to hinder the natural mobility of people on foot or bicycle. Such proposals are unlikely to make much of an impression on energy addicts and workaholics.

But they may intrigue others wanting to kick bad habits. However, if, above all, the task of living differently entails the task of thinking differently, then one must first escape the illusions fostered by such pop-scientific terms as "work" and "energy". To help with this, Illich favored thinking with concepts rooted in bodily experience. In contrast, transportation scientists have no concepts to distinguish biking under one's own power from being freighted in a bus. For them, both are comparable methods of locomotion. Social scientists define 'poverty' by the quantity of income. So understood, 'poverty' does not contrast the misery of those who are dependent on cash with the self-sufficiency of those who do not need it. Illich insisted on conceptual clarity rooted in felt perception as an antidote to the indiscriminating constructs of scientific thought.

These remarks do not summarize the four essays by Illich. Instead, they are invitations to rediscover a thinker who saw deeply into fundamental questions. Illich's texts demand and reward close attention.[1] In that effort, three misunderstandings should be avoided. First, only the inattentive reader will conclude that Illich was against technology per se. Such a reader must have misunderstood an argument built on defending, for example, bicycles, libraries, aspirin and books, all of which may use high-tech materials and industrial methods of production. A second and related confusion is to believe that Illich argued for the complete abolition of scarce commodities and services, whether computers or medicine: he simply insisted on discerning the quanta of commodities needed to expand the range of autarkic action, the proportion of power tools that would not destroy the use of one's hands. Third, one should guard against the idea that because he diagnosed the present from the vantage point of history, Illich was also calling for a return to the past. Instead, as he stated in *The Three Dimensions of Public Choice*, "such a choice does not exist", and such "aspirations ... would be sentimental and destructive". If he cautioned there is no way back, Illich also refused the seductions of futurists. These visionaries of freedom now promise redemption through a 'low carbon full employment' future. Forty years ago, Illich saw into that future and recognized there the tightening shackles of wages geared to watts.

Readers who share that recognition may be now prompted to laugh at the ardor of their attachment to false promises. That laughter may also liberate, in those who desire it, new efforts to invent and imagine ways of living that are truly free. To them, debates still tethered by expanding markets and powerful machines are irrelevant. They realize that the noisy discussions between proponents of "regulated" instead of "free" markets leave unquestioned the rule of scarce resources. They also see the confining grip of techno-science in claims that "sustainable technologies" will cure technologically caused damages. Moreover, those searching and inventing styles of living relatively free from the rule of economic value and techno-science are not doctrinaire. They know that the vernacular stubbornly persists in the interstices of contemporary life and lies orthogonally to commodity-intensive markets and energy-intensive machines. They stitch together, as in a patchwork quilt modes of life oriented by the homemade, homegrown, and homebred. They adroitly sidestep the charge of hypocrisy when leveled by those who disparage and repress vernacular ways. They leave purity of intent to the priests, definitional exactness to the academics, and despair to the intellectuals. Now freed of illusory attachments, they are too engaged in figuring out the shape of a sweeter, more beautiful life amidst the ruins bequeathed to them.

Valentina Borremans graciously gave me the permission to republish these essays. Catheryn Kilgarriff of Marion Boyars not only keeps many of Illich's books in print but also has been generous in her accommodation of missed deadlines. I am pleased to acknowledge John Verity's editorial suggestions that spurred me to rewrite this text. Carl Mitcham's suggestions helped polish it to the finish it now possesses. I remain grateful for the nourishing patience of Samar Farage. None of them is responsible for the remaining errors and infelicities.

Sajay Samuel
May 2013

---

1 *Ivan Illich in Conversation*, (Toronto: Anansi Press, 2002) remains the single best source to enter the thought of Illich at a leisurely pace. David Cayley, a master at his craft, conducts the conversation.

THE WAR AGAINST SUBSISTENCE

by Ivan Illich

HISTORIANS have chosen Columbus' voyage from Palos as a date convenient for marking the transition from the Middle Ages to modern times, a point useful for changing editors of textbooks. But the world of Ptolemy did not become the world of Mercator in one year, nor did the world of the vernacular become the age of education overnight. Rather, traditional cosmography was gradually adjusted in the light of widening experience. Columbus was followed by Cortéz, Copernicus by Kepler, Nebrija by Comenius. Unlike personal insight, the change in world view that generated our dependence on goods and services took 500 years.

How often the hand of the clock advances depends on the language of the ciphers on the quadrant. The Chinese speak of five stages in sprouting, and dawn approaches in seven steps for the Arabs. If I were to describe the evolution of *homo economicus* from Mandeville to Marx or Galbraith, I would come to a different view of epochs than if I had a mind to outline the stages in which the ideology of *homo educandus* developed from Nebrija through Radke to Comenius. And again, within this same paradigm, a different set of turning points would best describe the decay of untutored learning and the route toward the inescapable mis-education that educational institutions necessarily dispense.

It took a good decade to recognize that Columbus had found a new hemisphere, not just a new route. It took much longer to invent the concept 'New World' for the continent whose existence he had denied.

A full century and a half separated the claim of Nebrija – in the Queen's service he *had* to teach all her subjects to speak – and the claim of John Amos Comenius – the possession of a method by which an army of schoolteachers would teach every-body everything perfectly.

By the time of Comenius (1592–1670), the ruling groups of both the Old and New Worlds were deeply convinced of the need for such a method. An incident in the history of Harvard College aptly illustrates the point. On the one hundred and fiftieth birthday of Nebrija's grammar, John Winthrop, Jr. was on his way to Europe searching for a theologian and educator to accept the presidency of Harvard. One of the first persons he approached was the Czech Comenius, leader and last bishop of the Moravian Church. Winthrop found him in London, where he was organizing the Royal Society and advising the government on public schools. In *Magna Didactica, vel Ars Omnibus Omnia Omnino Docendi*, Comenius had succinctly defined the goals of his profession. Education begins in the womb and does not end until death. Whatever is worth knowing is worth teaching by a special method appropriate to the subject. The preferred world is the one so organized that it functions as a school for all. Only if learning is the result of teaching can individuals be raised to the fullness of their humanity. People who learn without being taught are more like animals than men. And the school system must be so organized that all, old and young, rich and poor, noble and low, men and women, be taught effectively, not just symbolically and ostentatiously.

These are the thoughts written by the potential president of Harvard. But he never crossed the Atlantic. By the time Winthrop met him, he had already accepted the invitation of the Swedish government to organize a national system of schools for Queen Christina. Unlike Nebrija, he never had to argue the need for his services – they were always in great demand. The domain of the vernacular, considered untouchable by Isabella, had become the hunting ground for job-seeking Spanish *letrados*, Jesuits, and Czech divines. A sphere of formal education had been disembedded. Formally taught mother tongue professionally handled according to abstract rules had begun to compare with and encroach upon the vernacular. This gradual replacement and degradation of the vernacular by its costly counterfeit heralds the coming of the market-intensive society in which we now live.

Vernacular comes from an Indo-Germanic root that implies 'rootedness' and 'abode'. *Vernaculum* as a Latin word was used for whatever was homebred, homespun, homegrown, home-made, as opposed to what was obtained in formal exchange. The child of one's slave and of one's wife, the donkey born of one's own beast, were vernacular beings, as was the staple that came from the garden or the commons. If Karl Polanyi had adverted to this fact, he might have used the term in the meaning accepted by the ancient Romans: sustenance derived from reciprocity patterns imbedded in every aspect of life, as distinguished from sustenance that comes from exchange or from vertical distribution.

Vernacular was used in this general sense from preclassical times down to the technical formulations found in the Codex of Theodosius. It was Varro who picked the term to introduce the same distinction in language. For him, *vernacular speech* is made up of the words and patterns grown on the speaker's own ground, as opposed to what is grown elsewhere and then transported. And since Varro's authority was widely recognized, his definition stuck. He was the librarian of both Caesar and Augustus and the first Roman to attempt a thorough and critical study of the Latin language. His *Lingua Latina* was a basic reference book for centuries. Quintillian admired him as the most learned of all Romans. And Quintillian, the Spanish-born drill master for the future senators of Rome, is always proposed to normal students as one of the founders of their profession. But neither can be compared to Nebrija. Both Varro and Quintillian were concerned with shaping the speech of senators and scribes, the speech of the forum. Not so Nebrija; he sought control in the Queen's name over the everyday speech of all her people. Simply, Nebrija proposed to substitute a mother tongue for the vernacular.

Vernacular came into English in the one restricted sense to which Varro had confined its meaning. Just now, I would like to resuscitate some of its old breath. We need a simple, straightforward word to designate the activities of people when they are not motivated by thoughts of exchange, a word that denotes autonomous, non-market related actions through which people satisfy everyday needs – the actions that by their own true nature escape bureaucratic control, satisfying needs to which, in the very process, they give specific shape. Vernacular seems a good old word for this purpose, and should be acceptable to many contemporaries. There are technical words that designate the satisfaction of needs that economists do not or cannot measure – social production as opposed to economic production, the generation of use-values as opposed to the production of commodities, household economics as opposed to market economics. But these terms are specialized, tainted with some ideological prejudice, and each, in a different way, badly limps. Each contrasting pair of terms, in its own way, also fosters the confusion that assigns vernacular undertakings to unpaid, standardized, formalized activities. It is this kind of confusion I wish to clarify. We need a simple adjective to name those acts of competence, lust, or concern that we want to defend from measurement or manipulation by Chicago Boys and Socialist Commissars. The term must be broad enough to fit the preparation of food and the shaping of language, childbirth and recreation, without implying either a privatized activity akin to the housework of modern women, a hobby or an irrational and primitive procedure. Such an adjective is not at hand. But 'vernacular' might serve. By speaking about vernacular language and the possibility of its recuperation, I am trying to bring into awareness and discussion the existence of a vernacular mode of being, doing, and making that in a desirable future society might again expand in all aspects of life.

Mother tongue, since the term was first used, has never meant the vernacular, but rather its contrary. The term was first used by Catholic monks to designate a particular language they used, instead of Latin, when speaking from the pulpit. No Indo-Germanic culture before had used the term. The word was introduced into Sanskrit in the eighteenth century as a translation from the English. The term has no roots in the other major language families now spoken on which I could check. The only classical people who viewed their homeland as a kind of mother were the Cretans. Bachofen suggests that memories of an old matriarchal order still lingered in their culture. But even in Crete, there was no equivalent to 'mother' tongue. To trace the association which led to the term *mother tongue*, I shall first have to look at what happened at the court of Charlemagne, and then what happened later in the Abbey of Gorz.

The idea that humans are born in such fashion that they need institutional service from professional agents in order to reach that humanity for which by birth all people are destined can be traced down to Carolingian times. It was then that, for the first time in history, it was discovered that there are certain basic needs, needs that are universal to mankind and that cry out for satisfaction in a standard fashion that cannot be met in a vernacular way. The discovery is perhaps best associated with the Church reform that took place in the eighth century. The Scottish monk Alcuin, the former chancellor of York University who became the court philosopher of Charles the Great, played a prominent role in this reform. Up to that time the Church had considered its ministers primarily as priests, that is, as men selected and invested with special powers to meet communitary, liturgical, public needs. They were engaged in preaching at ritual occasions and had to preside at functions. They acted as public officials, analogous to those others through whom the state provided for the administration of justice, or, in Roman times, for public work. To think of these kinds of magistrates as if they were 'service professionals' would be an anachronistic projection of our contemporary categories.

But then, from the eighth century on, the classical priest rooted in Roman and Hellenistic models began to be trans-mogrified into the precursor of the service professional: the teacher, social worker, or educator. Church ministers began to cater to the personal needs of parishioners and to equip them-selves with a sacramental and pastoral theology that defined and established these needs for their regular service. The institu-tionally defined care of the individual, the family, the village community, acquires unprecedented prominence. The term 'holy mother the church' ceases almost totally to mean the actual assembly of the faithful whose love, under the impulse of the Holy Spirit, engenders new life in the very act of meeting. The term *mother* henceforth refers to an invisible, mystical reality from which alone those services absolutely necessary for salva-tion can be obtained. Henceforth, access to the good graces of this mother on whom universally necessary salvation depends is entirely controlled by a hierarchy of ordained males. This gender-specific mythology of male hierarchies mediating access to the institutional source of life is without precedent. From the ninth to the eleventh century, the idea took shape that there are some needs common to all human beings that can be satisfied only through service from professional agents. Thus the definition of needs in terms of professionally defined commodities in the service sector precedes by a millennium the industrial production of universally needed basic goods.

Thirty-five years ago, Lewis Mumford tried to make this point. When I first read his statement that the monastic reform of the ninth century created some of the basic assumptions on which the industrial system is founded, I could not be convinced by something I considered more of an intuition than a proof. In the meantime, though, I have found a host of converging arguments – most of which Mumford does not seem to suspect – for rooting the ideologies of the industrial age in the earlier Carolingian Renaissance. The idea that there is no salvation without *personal services* provided by professionals in the name of an institutional Mother Church is one of these formerly unnoticed developments without which, again, our own age would be unthinkable. True, it took five hundred years of medieval theology to elaborate on this concept. Only by the end of the Middle Ages would the *pastoral* self-image of the Church be fully rounded. And only in the Council of Trent (1545) would this self-image of the Church as a mother milked by clerical hierarchies become formally defined. Then, in the *Constitution* of the Second Vatican Council (1964), the Catholic Church, which had served in the past as the prime model for the evolution of secular service organizations, aligns itself explicitly in the image of its secular imitations.

The important point here is the notion that the clergy can define its services as needs of human nature, and make this service-commodity the kind of necessity that cannot be forgone without jeopardy to eternal life. It is in this ability of a non-hereditary élite that we ought to locate the foundation without which the contemporary service or welfare state would not be conceivable. Surprisingly little research has been done on the religious concepts that fundamentally distinguish the industrial age from all other epochs. The official decline of the vernacular conception of Christian life in favor of one organized around pastoral care is a complex and drawn-out process constituting the background for a set of consistent shifts in the language and institutional development of the West.

When Europe first began to take shape as an idea and as a political reality, between Merovingian times and the High Middle Ages, what people spoke was unproblematic. It was called 'romance' or 'theodisc' – peoplish. Only somewhat later, *lingua vulgaris* became the common denominator distinguishing popular speech from the Latin of administration and doctrine. Since Roman times, a person's first language was the *patrius sermo*, the language of the male head of the household. Each such *sermo* or speech was perceived as a separate language. Neither in ancient Greece nor in the Middle Ages did people make the modern distinction between mutually understandable dialects and different languages. The same holds true today, for example, at the grass roots in India. What we know today as monolingual communities were and, in fact, are exceptions. From the Balkans to Indochina's western frontiers, it is still rare to find a village in which one cannot get along in more than two or three tongues. While it is assumed that each person has his *patrius sermo*, it is equally taken for granted that most persons speak several 'vulgar' tongues, each in a vernacular, untaught way. Thus the vernacular, in opposition to specialized, learned language – Latin for the Church, Frankish for the Court – was as obvious in its variety as the taste of local wines and food, as the shapes of house and hoe, down to the eleventh century. It is at this moment, quite suddenly, that the term *mother tongue* appears. It shows up in the sermons of some monks from the Abbey of Gorz. The process by which this phenomenon turns vernacular speech into a moral issue can only be touched upon here.

Gorz was a mother abbey in Lorraine, not far from Verdun. Benedictine monks had founded the monastery in the eighth century, around bones believed to belong to Saint Gorgonius. During the ninth century, a time of widespread decay in ecclesiastical discipline, Gorz, too, suffered a notorious decline. But only three generations after such scandalous dissolution Gorz became the center of monastic reform in the Germanic areas of the Empire. Its reinvigoration of Cistercian life paralleled the work of the reform abbey of Cluny. Within a century, 160 daughter abbeys throughout the northeastern parts of central Europe were established from Gorz.

It seems quite probable that Gorz was then at the center of the diffusion of a new technology that was crucial for the later imperial expansion of the European powers: the transformation of the horse into the tractor of choice. Four Asiastic inventions – the horseshoe, the fixed saddle and stirrup, the bit, and the cummett (the collar resting on the shoulder) – permitted important and extensive changes. One horse could replace six oxen. While supplying the same traction, and more speed, a horse could be fed on the acreage needed for one yoke of oxen. Because of its speed, the horse permitted a more extensive cultivation of the wet, northern soils, in spite of the short summers. Also, greater rotation of crops was possible. But even more importantly, the peasant could now tend fields twice as far away from his dwelling. A new pattern of life became possible. Formerly, people had lived in clusters of homesteads; now they could form villages large enough to support a parish and, later, a school. Through dozens of abbeys, monastic learning and discipline, together with the reorganization of settlement patterns, spread throughout this part of Europe.

Gorz lies close to the line that divides Frankish from Romance types of vernacular, and some monks from Cluny began to cross this line. In these circumstances, the monks of Gorz made language, vernacular language, into an issue to defend their territorial claims. The monks began to preach in Frankish, and spoke specifically about the value of the Frankish tongue. They began to use the pulpit as a forum to stress the importance of language itself, perhaps even to teach it. From the little we know, they used at least two approaches. First, Frankish was the language spoken by the women, even in those areas where the men were already beginning to use a Romance vernacular. Second, it was the language now used by Mother Church.

How charged with sacred meanings motherhood was in the religiosity of the twelfth century one can grasp through contemplating the contemporary statues of the Virgin Mary, or from reading the liturgical Sequences, the poetry of the time. The term mother tongue, from its very first use, instrumentalizes everyday language in the service of an institutional cause. The word was translated from Frankish into Latin. Then, as a rare Latin term, it incubated for several centuries. In the decades before Luther, quite suddenly and dramatically, mother tongue acquired a strong meaning. It came to mean the language created by Luther in order to translate the Hebrew Bible, the language taught by schoolmasters to read that book, and then the language that justified the existence of nation states.

Today, 'mother tongue' means several things: the first language learned by the child, and the language which the authorities of the state have decided ought to be one's first language. Thus, mother tongue can mean the first language picked up at random, generally a very different speech from the one taught by paid educators and by parents who act as if they were such educators. We see, then, that people are considered as creatures who need to be taught to speak properly in order 'to communicate' in the modern world – as they need to be wheeled about in motorized carriages in order to move in modern landscapes, their feet no longer fit. Dependence on taught mother tongue can be taken as the paradigm of all other dependencies typical of humans in an age of commodity-defined needs. And the ideology of this dependence was formulated by Nebrija. The ideology which claims that human mobility depends not on feet and open frontiers, but on the availability of 'transportation' is only slightly more than a hundred years old. Language teaching created employment long ago; macadam and the suspended coach made the conveyance of people a big business only from about the middle of the eighteenth century.

As language teaching has become a job, it has begun to cost a lot of money. Words are now one of the two largest categories of marketed values that make up the gross national product (GNP). Money decides what shall be said, who shall say it, when and what kind of people shall be targeted for the messages. The higher the cost of each uttered word, the more determined the echo demanded. In schools people learn to speak as they should. Money is spent to make the poor speak more like the wealthy, the sick more like the healthy; and the minority more like the majority. We pay to improve, correct, enrich, update the language of children and of their teachers. We spend more on the professional jargons that are taught in college, and more yet in high schools, to give teenagers a smattering of these jargons; but just enough to make them feel dependent on the psychologist, druggist, or librarian who is fluent in some special kind of English. We go even further: we first allow standard language to degrade ethnic, black, or hillbilly language, and then spend money to teach their counterfeits as academic subjects. Administrators and entertainers, admen and newsmen, ethnic politicians and 'radical' professionals, form powerful interest groups, each fighting for a larger slice of the language pie.

I do not really know how much is spent in the United States to make words. But soon someone will provide us with the necessary statistical tables. Ten years ago, energy accounting was almost unthinkable. Now it has become an established practice. Today you can easily look up how many 'energy units' have gone into growing, harvesting, packaging, transporting, and merchandising one edible calory of bread. The difference between the bread produced and eaten in a village in Greece and that found in an American supermarket is enormous – about forty times more energy units are contained in each edible calory of the latter. Bicycle traffic in cities permits one to move four times as fast as on foot for one-fourth of the energy expended – while cars, for the same progress, need 150 times as many calories per passenger mile. Information of this kind was available ten years ago, but no one thought about it. Today, it is recorded and will soon lead to a change in people's outlook on the need for fuels. It would now be interesting to know what language accounting looks like, since the linguistic analysis of contemporary language is certainly not complete, unless for each group of speakers we know the amount of money spent on shaping the speech of the average person. Just as social energy accounts are only approximate and at best allow us to identify the orders of magnitude within which the relative values are found, so language accounting would provide us with data on the relative prevalence of standardized, taught language in a population – sufficient, however, for the argument I want to make.

But mere per capita expenditure employed to mold the language of a group of speakers does not tell us enough. No doubt we would learn that each paid word addressed to the rich costs, per capita, much more than words addressed to the poor.

Watts are actually more democratic than words. But taught language comes in a vast range of qualities. The poor, for instance, are much more blared at than the rich, who can buy tutoring and, what is more precious, hedge on their own high class vernacular by purchasing silence. The educator, politician and entertainer now come with a loudspeaker to Oaxaca, to Travancore, to the Chinese commune, and the poor immediately forfeit the claim to that indispensable luxury, the silence out of which vernacular language arises.

Yet even without putting a price-tag on silence, even without the more detailed language economics on which I would like to draw, I can still estimate that the dollars spent to power any nation's motors pale before those that are now expended on prostituting speech in the mouths of paid speakers. In rich nations, language has become incredibly spongy, absorbing huge investments. Generous expenditure to cultivate the language of the mandarin, the author, the actor, or the charmer have always been a mark of high civilization. But these were efforts to teach élites special codes. Even the cost of making some people learn secret languages in traditional societies is incomparably lower than the capitalization of language in industrial societies.

In poor countries today, people still speak to each other without the experience of capitalized language, although such countries always contain a tiny élite who manage very well to allocate a larger proportion of the national income for their prestige language. Let me ask: What is different in the everyday speech of groups whose language has received – or shall I say absorbed? resisted? survived? suffered? enjoyed? – huge investments, and the speech of people whose language has remained outside the market? Comparing these two worlds of language, I want to focus my curiosity on just one issue that arises in this context. Does the structure and function of the language itself change with the rate of investment? Are these alterations such that all languages that absorb funds show changes in the same direction? In this introductory exploration of the subject, I cannot demonstrate that this is the case. But I do believe my arguments make both propositions highly probable, and show that structurally oriented language economics are worth exploring.

Taught everyday language is without precedent in pre-industrial cultures. The current dependence on paid teachers and models of ordinary speech is just as much a unique characteristic of industrial economies as dependence on fossil fuels. The need for taught mother tongue was discovered four centuries earlier, but only in our generation have both language and energy been effectively treated as worldwide needs to be satisfied for all people by planned, programmed production and distribution. Because, unlike the vernacular of capitalized language, we can reasonably say that it results from *production*.

Traditional cultures subsisted on sunshine, which was captured mostly through agriculture. The hoe, the ditch, the yoke, were basic means to harness the sun. Large sails or waterwheels were known, but rare. These cultures that lived mostly on the sun subsisted basically on vernacular values. In such societies, tools were essentially the prolongation of arms, fingers, and legs. There was no need for the production of power in centralized plants and its distant distribution to clients. Equally, in these essentially sun-powered cultures, there was no need for language production. Language was drawn by each one from the cultural environment, learned from the encounter with people whom the learner could smell and touch, love or hate. The vernacular spread just as most things and services were shared, namely, by multiple forms of mutual reciprocity, rather than clientage to the appointed teacher or professional. Just as fuel was not delivered, so the vernacular was never taught. Taught tongues did exist, but they were rare, as rare as sails and sills. In most cultures, we know that speech resulted from conversation embedded in everyday life, from listening to fights and lullabies, gossip, stories, and dreams. Even today, the majority of people in poor countries learn all their language skills without any paid tutorship, without any attempt whatsoever to teach them how to speak. And they learn to speak in a way that nowhere compares with the self-conscious, self-important, colorless mumbling that, after a long stay in villages in South America and Southeast Asia, always shocks me when I visit an American college. I feel sorrow for those students whom education has made tone deaf; they have lost the faculty for hearing the difference between the dessicated utterance of standard television English and the living speech of the un-schooled. What else can I expect, though, from people who are not brought up at a mother's breast, but on formula? On canned milk, if they are from poor families, and on a brew prepared under the nose of Ralph Nader if they are born among the enlightened? For people trained to choose between packaged formulas, mother's breast appears as just one more option. And in the same way, for people who were intentionally *taught* to listen and to speak, untutored vernacular seems just like another, albeit less developed, model among many.

But this is simply false. Language exempt from rational tutor-ship is a different kind of social phenomenon from language that is purposefully taught. Where untutored language is the predominant marker of a shared world, a sense of power within the group exists, and this sense cannot be duplicated by lan-guage that is delivered. One way this difference shows is the sense of power over language itself, over its acquisition. Even today, the poor in non-industrial countries all over the world are polyglot. My friend, the goldsmith in Timbuktu, speaks Songhay at home, listens to Bambara on the radio, devotedly and with some understanding says his prayers five times a day in Arabic, gets along in two trade languages on the Souk, con-verses in passable French that he picked up in the army – and none of these languages was formally taught him. He did not set out to learn these tongues; each is one style in which he remembers a peculiar set of experiences that fits into the frame of that language. Communities in which monolingual people prevail are rare except in three kinds of settings: tribal com-munities that have not really experienced the late neolithic, communities that for a long time lived through exceptional forms of discrimination, and among the citizens of nation states that, for several generations, have enjoyed the benefits of com-pulsory schooling. To take it for granted that most people are monolingual is typical of the members of the middle class. Admiration for the vernacular polyglot unfailingly exposes the social climber.

Throughout history, untutored language was prevalent, but it was hardly ever the only kind of language known. Just as in traditional cultures some energy was captured through wind-mills and canals, and those who had large boats or those who cornered the right spot on the brook could use their tool for a net transfer of power to their own advantage, so some people have always used a taught language to corner some privilege. But such additional codes remained either rare and special, or served very narrow purposes. The ordinary language, until Nebrija, was prevalently vernacular. And this vernacular, be it the ordinary colloquial, a trade idiom, the language of prayer, the craft jargon, the language of basic accounts, the language of venery or of age (for example, baby talk) was learned on the side, as part of meaningful everyday life. Of course, Latin or Sanskrit were formally taught to the priest, court languages such as Frankish or Persian or Turkish were taught to the future scribe. Neophytes were formally initiated into the language of astronomy, alchemy, or late masonry. And, clearly, the knowledge of such formally taught languages raised a man above others, somewhat like the saddle lifts the free man above the serfs in the infantry, or the bridge lifts the captain above the crew. But even when access to some élite language was unlocked by a formal initiation, it did not necessarily mean that language was being taught. Quite frequently, the process of formal initiation did not transfer to the initiate a new language skill, but simply exempted him henceforth from a taboo that forbade others to use certain words, or to speak out on certain occasions. Male initiation in the language of the hunt or of sex is probably the most widespread example of such a ritually selective language de-tabooization.

But, in traditional societies, no matter how much or how little language was taught, the taught language rarely rubbed off on vernacular speech. Neither the existence of some language teaching at all times nor the spread of some language through professional preachers or comedians weakens my main point: outside of those societies that we now call Modern European, no attempt was made to impose on entire populations an everyday language that would be subject to the control of paid teachers or announcers. Everyday language, until recently, was nowhere the product of design; it was nowhere paid for and delivered like a commodity. And while every historian who deals with the origins of nation states pays attention to the imposition of a national tongue, economists generally overlook the fact that this taught mother tongue is the earliest of specifically modern commodities, the model of all 'basic needs' to come.

Before I can go on to contrast taught colloquial speech and vernacular speech, costly language and that which comes at no cost, I must clarify one more distinction. Between taught mother tongue and the vernacular I draw the line of demarcation somewhere else than linguists when they distinguish the high language of an élite from the dialect spoken in lower classes, somewhere other than the frontier that separates regional and superregional languages, somewhere else than restricted and corrected code, and somewhere else than at the line between the language of the literate and the illiterate. No matter how restricted within geographic boundaries, no matter how distinctive for a social level, no matter how specialized for one sex role or one caste, language can be either vernacular (in the sense in which I here use the term) or of the taught variety. Elite language, trade language, second language, local idiom, are nothing new. But each of these can be formally taught and the taught counterfeit of the vernacular comes as a commodity and is something entirely new.

The contrast between these two complementary forms is most marked and important in taught everyday language, that is, taught colloquial, taught standardized everyday speech. But here again we must avoid confusion. Not all standard language is either grammar-ridden or taught. In all of history, one mutually understandable dialect has tended toward predominance in a given region. This kind of principal dialect was often accepted as the standard form. It was indeed written more frequently than other dialects, but not, for that reason, was it taught. Rather, diffusion occurred through a much more complex and subtle process. Midland English, for example, slowly emerged as that second, common style in which people born into any English dialect could also speak their own tongue. Quite suddenly, the language of Mogul hordes (Urdu) came into being in northern India. Within two generations, it became the standard in Hindustan, the trade language in a vast area, and the medium for exquisite poetry written in the Arabic and Sanskrit alphabets. Not only was this language not taught for several generations, but poets who wanted to perfect their competence explicitly avoided the study of Hindu-Urdu; they explored the Persian, Arabic, or Sanskrit sources that had originally contributed to its being. In Indonesia, in half a generation of resistance to Japanese and Dutch, the militant fraternal and combative slogans, posters, and secret radios of the freedom struggle spread Malay competence into every village, and did so much more effectively than the later efforts of the Ministry of Language Control that was established after independence.

It is true that the dominant position of élite or standard language was always bolstered by the technique of writing. Printing enormously enhanced the colonizing power of élite language. But to say that because printing was invented élite language is destined to supplant vernacular variety results from a debilitated imagination – like saying that after the atom bomb only super powers shall be sovereign. The historical monopoly of educational bureaucracies over the printing press is no argument that printing techniques cannot be used to give new vitality to written expression and new literary opportunity to thousands of vernacular forms. The fact that the printing press could augment the extent and power of ungovernable vernacular readings was the source of Nebrija's greatest concern and of his argument *against* the vernacular. The fact that printing was used since the early sixteenth century (but not during the first forty years of its existence) primarily for the imposition of standard colloquials does not mean that printed language must always be a taught form. The commercial status of taught mother tongue, call it national language, literary standard, or television language, rests largely on unexamined axioms, some of which I have already mentioned: that printing implies standardized composition; that books written in the standard language could not be easily read by people who had not been schooled in that tongue; that reading is by its very nature a silent activity that usually should be conducted in private; that enforcing a universal ability to read a few sentences and then copy them in writing increases the access of a population to the content of libraries: these and other such illusions are used to enhance the standing of teachers, the sale of rotary presses, the grading of people according to their language code and, up to now, an increase in the GNP.

Vernacular spreads by practical use; it is learned from people who mean what they say and who say what they mean to the person they address in the context of everyday life. This is not so in taught language. With taught language, the one from whom I learn is not a person whom I care for or dislike, but a professional speaker. The model for taught colloquial is somebody who does not say what he means, but who recites what others have contrived. In this sense, a street vendor announcing his wares in ritual language is not a professional speaker, while the King's herald or the clown on television are the prototypes. Taught colloquial is the language of the announcer who follows the script that an editor was told by a publicist that a board of directors had decided should be said. Taught colloquial is the dead, impersonal rhetoric of people paid to declaim with phony conviction texts composed by others, who themselves are usually paid only for *designing* the text. People who speak taught language imitate the announcer of news, the comedian of gag writers, the instructor following the teacher's manual to explain the textbook, the songster of engineered rhymes, or the ghost-written president. This is language that implicitly lies when I use it to say something to your face; it is meant for the spectator who watches the scene. It is the language of farce, not of theater, the language of the hack, not of the true performer. The language of the media always seeks the appropriate audience profile that the sponsor tries to hit and to hit hard. While the vernacular is engendered in me by the intercourse between complete persons locked in conversation with each other, taught language is syntonic with loudspeakers whose assigned job is gab.

The vernacular and taught mother tongue are like the two extremes on the spectrum of the colloquial. Language would be totally inhuman if it were totally taught. That is what Humboldt meant when he said that real language is speech that can only be fostered, never taught like mathematics. Speech is much more than communication, and only machines can communicate without reference to vernacular roots. Their chatter with one another in New York now takes up about three-quarters of the lines that the telephone company operates under a franchise that guarantees access by people. This is an obvious perversion of a legal privilege that results from political aggrandizement and the degradation of vernacular domains to second-class commodities. But even more embarrassing and depressing than this abuse of a forum of free speech by robots is the incidence of robot-like stock phrases that blight the remaining lines on which people presumably 'speak' to each other. A growing percentage of speech has become mere formula in content and style. In this way, the colloquial moves on the spectrum of language increasingly from vernacular to capital-intensive 'communication', as if it were nothing more than the human variety of the exchange that also goes on between bees, whales, and computers. True, some vernacular elements or aspects always survive – but that is the case even for most computer programs. I do not claim that the vernacular dies; only that it withers. The American, French, or German colloquials have become composites made up of two kinds of language: commodity-like taught uniquack and a limping, ragged, jerky vernacular struggling to survive. Taught mother tongue has established a radical monopoly over speech, just as transportation has over mobility or, more generally, commodity over vernacular values.

A resistance, sometimes as strong as a sacred taboo, prevents people shaped by life in industrial society from recognizing the difference with which we are dealing – the difference between capitalized language and the vernacular, which comes at no economically measurable cost. It is the same kind of inhibition that makes it difficult for those who are brought up within the industrial system to sense the fundamental distinction between nurture from the breast and feeding by bottle, between literature and textbook, between a mile moved on my own and a passenger mile – areas where I have discussed this issue over the past years.

Most people would probably be willing to admit that there is a huge difference in taste, meaning, and satisfaction between a home-cooked meal and a TV dinner. But the examination and understanding of this difference can be easily blocked, especially among those committed to equal rights, equity and service to the poor. They know how many mothers have no milk in their breasts, how many children in the South Bronx suffer protein deficiencies, how many Mexicans – surrounded by fruit trees – are crippled by vitamin deficits. As soon as I raise the distinction between vernacular values and values susceptible of economic measurement and, therefore, of being administered, some self-appointed tutor of the so-called proletariat will tell me that I am avoiding the critical issue by giving importance to non-economic niceties. Should we not seek first the just distribution of commodities that correlate to basic needs? Poetry and fishing shall then be added without more thought or effort. So goes the reading of Marx and the Gospel of St. Matthew as interpreted by the theology of liberation.

A laudable intention here attempts an argument that should have been recognized as illogical in the nineteenth century, and that countless experiences have shown false in the twentieth. So far, every single attempt to substitute a universal commodity for a vernacular value has led, not to equality, but to a hier-archical modernization of poverty. In the new dispensation, the poor are no longer those who survive by their vernacular activi-ties because they have only marginal or no access to the market. No, the modernized poor are those whose vernacular domain, in speech and in action, is most restricted – those who get least satisfaction out of the few vernacular activities in which they can still engage.

The second-level taboo which I have set out to violate is not constituted by the distinction between the vernacular and taught mother tongue, nor by the destruction of the vernacular through the radical monopoly of taught mother tongue over speech, nor even by the class-biased intensity of this vernacular paralysis. Although these three matters are far from being clearly understood today, they have been widely discussed in the recent past. The point at issue which is sedulously over-looked is quite another: Mother tongue is taught increasingly, not by paid agents, but by unpaid parents. These latter deprive their own children of the last opportunity to listen to adults who have something to say to each other. This was brought home to me clearly, some time ago, while back in New York City in an area that a few decades earlier I had known quite well, the South Bronx. I went there at the request of a young college teacher, married to a colleague. This man wanted my signature on a petition for compensatory pre-kindergarten language training for the inhabitants of a partially burnt-out, high-rise slum. Twice already, quite decidedly and yet with deep em-barrassment, I had refused. To overcome my resistance against this expansion of educational services, he took me on visits to brown, white, black, mostly single-parent so-called households. I saw dozens of children dashing through uninhabitable cement corridors, exposed all day to blaring television and radio in English, Spanish and even Yiddish. They seemed equally lost in language and landscape. As my friend pressed for my signature, I tried to argue for the protection of these children against further castration and inclusion in the educational sphere. We talked at cross-purposes, unable to meet. And then, in the evening, at dinner in my friend's home, I suddenly understood why. This man, whom I viewed with awe because he had chosen to live in this hell, had ceased to be a parent and had become a total teacher. In front of their own children this couple stood *in loco magistri*. Their children had to grow up without parents, because these two adults, in every word they addressed to their two sons and one daughter, were 'educating' them – they were at dinner constantly conscious that they were modeling the speech of their children, and they asked me to do the same.

For the professional parent who engenders children as a professional lover, who volunteers his semi-professional counseling skills for neighborhood organizations, the distinction between his unpaid contribution to the managed society and what could be, in contrast, the recovery of vernacular domains, remains meaningless. He is fit prey for a new type of growth-oriented ideology – the planning and organization of an expanding shadow economy, the last frontier of arrogance which *homo economicus* faces.

SHADOW WORK

by Ivan Illich

NADINE GORDIMER's novel *Burger's Daughter*, was on my desk as I began to outline this essay. With rare discipline, she reflects our age's liberal arrogance in the shameless, brilliant mirror of her homeland, the South African police state. Her protagonist suffers from an 'illness' – "not to be able to ignore that condition of a healthy, ordinary life: other people's suffering." In *The Feminization of America*, Ann Douglas makes a similar point. For her, the illness is the loss of sentimentality, a sentimentality asserting that the values which industrial society destroys are precisely those which it cherishes. There is no known substitute for this dishonesty in an industrial society. Those affected by the loss of sentimentality become aware of apartheid: that which we have now, or that which we shall get after the revolution.

In this essay, I want to explore why, in an industrial society, this apartheid is unavoidable; why without apartheid based on sex or pigmentation, on certification or race, or party membership, a society built on the assumption of scarcity cannot exist. And to approach the unexamined forms of apartheid in concrete terms, I want to speak about the fundamental bifurcation of work that is implicit in the industrial mode of production.

I have chosen as my theme the shady side of the industrial economy and, more specifically, the shady side of work. I do not mean badly paid work, nor unemployment; I mean unpaid work. The unpaid work which is unique to the industrial economy is my theme. In most societies men and women together have maintained and regenerated the subsistence of their households by unpaid activities. The household itself created most of what it needed to exist. These so-called subsistence activities are not my subject. My interest is in that entirely different form of unpaid work which an industrial society demands as a necessary complement to the production of goods and services. This kind of unpaid servitude does not contribute to subsistence. Quite the contrary, equally with wage labor, it ravages subsistence. I call this complement to wage labor 'shadow work'. It comprises most housework women do in their homes and apartments, the activities connected with shopping, most of the homework of students cramming for exams, the toil expended commuting to and from the job. It includes the stress of forced consumption, the tedious and regimented surrender to therapists, compliance with bureaucrats, the preparation for work to which one is compelled, and many of the activities usually labelled 'family life'.

In traditional cultures the shadow work is as marginal as wage labor, often difficult to identify. In industrial societies, it is assumed as routine. Euphemism, however, scatters it. Strong taboos act against its analysis as a unified entity. Industrial production determines its necessity, extent and forms. But it is hidden by the industrial-age ideology, according to which all those activities into which people are coerced for the sake of the economy, by means that are primarily social, count as satisfaction of needs rather than as work.

To grasp the nature of shadow work we must avoid two confusions. It is not a subsistence activity; it feeds the formal economy, not social subsistence. Nor is it underpaid wage labor; its unpaid performance is the condition for wages to be paid. I shall insist on the distinction between shadow and subsistence work, as much as on its distinction from wage labor, no matter how vigorous the protests from unionists, marxists and some feminists. I shall examine shadow work as a unique form of bondage, not much closer to servitude than to either slavery or wage labor.

While for wage labor you apply and qualify, to shadow work you are born or are diagnosed for. For wage labor you are selected; into shadow work you are put. The time, toil and loss of dignity entailed are exacted without pay. Yet increasingly the unpaid self-discipline of shadow work becomes more important than wage labor for further economic growth.

In advanced industrial economies these unpaid contributions toward economic growth have become the social locus of the most widespread, the most unchallenged, the most depressing form of discrimination. Shadow work, unnamed and un-examined, has become the principal area of discrimination against the majority in every industrial society. It cannot be ignored much longer. The amount of shadow work laid on a person today is a much better measure of discrimination than bias on the job. Rising unemployment and rising productivity combine now to create an increasing need to diagnose ever more people for shadow work. The 'age of leisure', the 'age of self-help', the 'service economy', are euphemisms for this grow-ing specter. To fully comprehend the nature of shadow work, I shall trace its history, a history which runs parallel to that of wage labor.

Both 'work' and 'job' are key words today. Neither had its present prominence three hundred years ago. Both are still un-translatable from European languages into many others. Most languages never had one single word to designate all activities that are considered useful. Some languages happen to have a word for activities demanding pay. This word usually connotes graft, bribery, tax or extortion of interest payments. None of these words would comprehend what we call 'work'.

For the last three decades, the Ministry for Language Development in Djakarta tried to impose the one term *bekerdja* in lieu of half a dozen others used to designate productive jobs. Sukarno had considered this monopoly of one term a necessary step for creating a Malay working class. The language planners got some compliance from journalists and union leaders. But the people continue to refer to what they do with different terms for pleasurable, or degrading, or tiresome, or bureaucratic actions – whether they are paid or not. All over Latin America, people find it easier to perform the paid task assigned to them than to grasp what the boss means by *trabajo*. For most toiling unem-ployed in Mexico, *desempleado* still means the unoccupied loafer on a well-paid job, not the unemployed whom the economist means by the term.

For classical Greeks or later Romans, work done with the hands, done under orders or involving income from trade was servile, better left to the lowly or slaves. In theory, Christians should have considered labor as part of each man's vocation. Paul, the tentmaker, had tried to introduce the Jewish work ethic into early Christianity: "who does not work shall not eat". In fact, though, this early Christian ideal was very thoroughly repressed. In Western monasteries, except for short periods of reform, the monks interpreted St. Benedict's motto 'ora et labora' as a call to supervise lay brothers at work, and to do God's work by prayer. Neither the Greeks nor the Middle Ages had a term resembling our work or job.

What today stands for work, namely, wage labor, was a badge of misery all through the Middle Ages. It stood in clear opposition to at least three other types of toil: the activities of the household by which most people subsisted, quite marginal to any money economy; the trades of people who made shoes, barbered or cut stones; the various forms of beggary by which people lived on what others shared with them. In principle, medieval society provided a berth for everyone whom it recognized as a member – its structural design excluded unemployment and destitution. When one engaged in wage labor, not occasionally as the member of a household but as a regular means of total support, he clearly signaled to the community that he, like a widow or an orphan, had no berth, no household, and so stood in need of public assistance.

In September of 1330 a rich cloth merchant died in Florence and left his property to be distributed among the destitute. The Guild of Or San Michele was to administer the estate. The 17,000 beneficiaries were selected and locked into the available churches at midnight. As they were let out, each received his inheritance. Now, how were these 'destitute' selected? We know, because we have access to the welfare notes of Or San Michele Guild in proto-industrial Florence. From it, we know the categories of the destitute: orphan, widow, victim of a recent act of God, heads of family totally dependent on wage work, or those compelled to pay rent for the roof over their bed. The need to provide for all the necessities of life by wage work was a sign of utter impotence in an age when poverty designated primarily a valued attitude rather than an economic condition. The pauper was opposed to the *potens*, the powerful, not yet to the *dives*, the rich. Until the late twelfth century, the term poverty designated primarily a realistic detachment from transitory things. The need to live by wage labor was the sign for the down and out, for those too wretched to be simply added to that huge medieval crowd of cripples, exiles, pilgrims, madmen, friars, ambulants, homeless that made up the world of the poor. The dependence on wage labor was the recognition that the worker did not have a home where he could contribute within the household. The right to beggary was a normative issue, but never the right to work.

To clarify the right to beggary, let me quote from a sermon by Ratger of Verona, preached nearly half a millenium earlier than the Florentine example. The sermon was delivered in 834 and is a moral exhortation on the rights and duties of beggars.

> You complain about your weakness. Rather thank God, do not complain, and pray for those who keep you alive. And you, over there, healthy though you are, complain about the burden of your large brood. Then abstain from your wife, but not without first getting her agreement, and work with your hands so that you can feed yourself and others. You say you cannot do this. Then cry about your own weakness, which is burdensome for you. Beg with restraint for what is necessary, abstain from all that is superfluous . . . Keep company with the sick, succor the dying and wash the dead.

Ratger here speaks about a right to beggary that for a thousand years was never challenged.

The abhorrence of wage labor still fits the outlook which might be shared by today's world majority. But with the current dominance of economics in everyday language, people lack the words to express their feelings directly. In a letter I received from a 23-year old Mexican, a kind of wonderment for those totally dependent on wage labor comes through clearly. Miguel is the son of a widow who brought up four children by growing radishes and selling them from a *petate* on the floor of the local market. Besides the children, there were always some outsiders eating or sleeping at her home. Miguel went to Germany as the guest of Mr. Mueller, a grade school teacher in his native village, who in five years had renovated part of an old house, adding a guest room. Miguel accepted the invitation in order to obtain training in art photography from Leitz. He wants to document traditional weaving techniques.

Unhampered by previous schooling, Miguel quickly learned to speak German. But he had difficulties understanding the people. In his letter, written after six months in Germany, he reported: "Señor Mueller behaves as *todo un senor* [a true gentleman might be the English equivalent]. But most Germans act like destitute people with too much money. No one can help another. No one can take people in – into his household." I believe that Miguel's comments reflect well the situation and attitudes of a past millenium: people who live on wages have no subsistent household, are deprived of the means to provide for their subsistence and feel impotent to offer any subsistence to others. For Miguel, wage labor has not yet gotten stuck beyond the looking glass.

But for most people in Europe and the West, wage labor went through the looking glass between the seventeenth and nineteenth century. Instead of being a proof of destitution, wages came to be perceived as a proof of usefulness. Rather than being a supplement to subsistent existence, wages came to be viewed – by those who paid them – as the natural source of livelihood for a population. These populations had been excluded from the means of subsistence by progressive forms of enclosures. An incident illustrates the beginning of this process. In 1777, barely twelve years before the Revolution, the Academy of Chalon-sur-Marne in Northwest France endowed a competition for the best treatment of the following problem: how to abolish rampant beggary in ways that would profit the Crown and be in the interest of the poor. The initiative reflects the increase of beggary in an age of enclosure, proto-industry and bourgeois values. It also reflects a new economic meaning of poverty, a condition now opposed, not to the powerful, but to the moneyed. The prize for the competition was awarded an essay whose opening sentences sum up its thesis: "For centuries, people have searched for the stone of wisdom. We have found it. It is work. Wage labor is the natural source of enrichment for the poor."

The author is certainly a man of letters, a clerk. He probably lives on some sinecure, a benefice or some other form of handout. To his own mental labors, he would never attribute such wondrous transforming powers. He would insist on his right to high-class beggary. He is a modern professor, who believes himself a white collar worker, justly earning his living, being socially productive. But for both, it would be true to say: those who since the eighteenth century write about work, its value, dignity, pleasures, always write about the work that others do.

The text also reflects the influence of hermetic or alchemic thought on social theory. Work is presented as the stone of wisdom, the panacea, the magic elixir which transforms what it touches into gold. Nature turns into priced goods and services by its contact with the labor which transmutes it. Making various concessions for the contribution of capital and resources to value, this is the fundamental position of classical economists from Adam Smith and Ricardo to Mill and Marx. The alchemic language of the late eighteenth century was replaced by Marx with the then fashionable 'coquetry', the language of chemistry. The hermetic perception of value has continued to determine the character of social ethics until today, even though the labor theory of value was replaced, in economics, first by utility theory, then by post-Keynesian thought, and finally by the utter confusion which attends the contemporary insight that "economists conceive of the world in terms that fail to grasp its essential characteristics or that seriously misrepresent them." Economists understand about work about as much as alchemists about gold.

The prize-winning essay of 1777 is also remarkable for the late date at which, in France, the policy to compel the poor to useful work was considered a novelty. Until the mid-eighteenth century, French poorhouses were run on the medieval Christian assumption that forced labor was a punishment for sin or crime. In protestant Europe and in some Italian cities which were industrialized early, that view had been abandoned a century earlier. The pioneering policies and equipment in Dutch Calvinist or North German workhouses clearly show this. They were organized and equipped for the cure of laziness and for the development of the will to do work as assigned. These workhouses were designed and built to transform useless beggars into useful workers. As such, they were the reverse of medieval alms-giving agencies. Set up to receive beggars caught by the police, these institutions softened them up for treatment by a few days of no food and a carefully planned ration of daily lashes. Then, treatment with work at the treadmill or at the rasp followed until the transformation of the inmate into a useful worker was diagnosed. One even finds provisions for intensive care. People resistant to work were thrown into a constantly flooding pit, where they could survive only by frantically pumping all day long. Not only in their pedagogical approach, but also in their method of training for self-approbation, these institutions are true precursors of compulsory schools. In 1612, only seventeen years after the foundation of the Amsterdam Workhouse, one of the regents published, tongue in cheek, a report on two dozen miraculous therapeutic successes. Each one purports to be the grateful acknowledgment of a cure from sloth by a successfully treated (schooled) patient. Even if these are authentic, they certainly do not reflect popular sentiment. The destitute of the eighteenth century, by this date generally labelled as the 'poor', violently resisted such efforts to qualify them for work. They sheltered and defended those whom the police tried to classify as 'beggars' and whom the government tried to cure of social uselessness in order to protect the unobtrusive poor from such vagrants.

Even the harshest governments seemed unsuccessful in their forays. The crowd remained ungovernable. The Prussian Secretary of the Interior, in 1747, threatens severe punishment to anyone who interferes with the poverty-police:

> . . . from morning till night, we try to have this police cruise through our streets to stop beggary . . . but as soon as soldiers, commoners or the crowd notice the arrest of a beggar to bring him to the poorhouse, they riot, beat up our officers sometimes hurting them grievously and liberate the beggar. It has become almost impossible to get the poverty-police to take to the street . . .

Seven more analogous decrees were issued during the following thirty years.

All through the eighteenth and well into the nineteenth century, the project of Economic Alchemy produced no echo from below. The plebeians rioted. They rioted for just grain prices, they rioted against the export of grain from their regions, they rioted to protect prisoners of debt and felt protected whenever the law seemed not to coincide with their tradition of natural justice. The proto-industrial plebian crowd defended its 'moral economy' as Thompson has called it. And they rioted against the attacks on this economy's social foundation: against the enclosure of sheep and now against the enclosure of beggars. And in these riots, the crowd was led, more often than not, by its women. How did this rioting proto-industrial crowd, defending its right to subsistence turn into a striking labor force, defending 'rights' to wages? What was the social device that did the job, where the new poor laws and workhouses had failed? It was the economic division of labor into a productive and a non-productive kind, pioneered and first enforced through the domestic enclosure of women.

An unprecedented economic division of the sexes, an unprecedented economic conception of the family, an unprecedented antagonism between the domestic and public spheres made wage work into a necessary adjunct of life. All this was accomplished by making working men into the wardens of their domestic women, one on one, and making this guardianship into a burdensome duty. The enclosure of women succeeded where the enclosure of sheep and beggars had failed.

Why the struggle for subsistence was so suddenly abandoned and why this demise went unnoticed, can be understood only by bringing to light the concurrent creation of shadow work and the theory that woman, by her scientifically discovered nature, was destined to do it. While men were encouraged to revel in their new vocation to the working class, women were surreptitiously redefined as the ambulant, full-time matrix of society. Philosophers and physicians combined to enlighten society about the true nature of woman's body and soul. This new conception of her 'nature' destined her for activities in a kind of home which discriminated against her wage labor as effectively as it precluded any real contribution to the household's subsistence. In practice, the labor theory of value made man's work into the catalyst of gold, and degraded the homebody into a housewife economically dependent and, as never before, unproductive. She was now man's beautiful property and faithful support needing the shelter of home for her labor of love.

The bourgeois war on subsistence could enlist mass support only when the plebeian rabble turned into a clean-living working class made up of economically distinct men and women. As a member of this class, the man found himself in a conspiracy with his employer – both were equally concerned with economic expansion and the suppression of subsistence. Yet this fundamental collusion between capital and labor in the war on subsistence was mystified by the ritual of class struggle. Simultaneously man, as head of a family increasingly dependent on his wages, was urged to perceive himself burdened with all society's legitimate work, and under constant extortion from an unproductive woman. In and through the family the two complementary forms of industrial work were now fused: wage work and shadow work. Man and woman, both effectively estranged from subsistence activities, became the motive for the other's exploitation for the profit of the employer and investments in capital goods. Increasingly, surplus was not invested only in the so-called means of production. Shadow work itself became more and more capital-intensive. Investments in the home, the garage and the kitchen reflect the disappearance of subsistence from the household, and the evidence of a growing monopoly of shadow work. Yet this shadow work has been consistently mystified. Four such mystifications are still current today.

The first comes masked as an appeal to biology. It describes the relegation of women to the role of mothering housewives as a universal and necessary condition to allow men to hunt for the prey of the job. Four modern disciplines seem to legitimate this assumption. Ethologists describe female apes like housewives guarding the nest, while the males hunt through the trees. From this projection of family roles onto the ape, they infer that nesting is the gender specific role of the female and real work, that is, the conquest of scarce resources, is the task of the male. The myth of the mighty hunter is then by them defined as a cross-cultural constant, a behavioral bedrock of humanoids, derived from some biological substratum of higher mammals. Anthropologists irresistibly rediscover among savages the traits of their own moms and dads, and find features of the apartments in which they were bred, in tents, huts and caves. From hundreds of cultures, they gather evidence that women were always handicaped by their sex, good for digging rather than hunting, guardians of the home. Sociologists, like Parsons, start from the functions they believe to discern in today's family and then let the gender-roles within the family illuminate the other structures of society. Finally, sociobiologists of the right and the left give a contemporary veneer to the enlightenment myth that female behavior is male adaptive.

Common to all these is a basic confusion between the gender-specific assignment of tasks that is characteristic for each culture, and the uniquely modern economic bifurcation in nineteenth century work ideology that establishes a previously unknown apartheid between the sexes: he, primarily the producer; she, primarily private-domestic. This economic distinction of sex-roles was impossible under conditions of subsistence. It uses mystified tradition to legitimate the growing distinction of consumption and production by *defining what women do as non-work*.

The second mask for shadow work confuses it with 'social reproduction'. This latter term is an unfortunate category that Marxists use to label sundry activities which do not fit their ideology of work, but which must be done by someone – for example, keeping house for the wage worker. It is carelessly applied to what most people did most of the time in most societies, that is, subsistence activities. Also, it named activities that in the late nineteenth century were still considered to be non-productive wage labor, the work of teachers or social workers. Social reproduction includes most of what all people do around the home today. The label thus thwarts every attempt to grasp the difference between woman's basic and vital contribution to a subsistence economy, and her unpaid conscription into the reproduction of industrial labor – *unproductive women are consoled with 're-production'*.

The third device that masks shadow work is the assignment of shadow prices to sundry behavior outside the monetary market. All unpaid activities are amalgamated into a so-called informal sector. While the old economists built their theory on the foregone conclusion that every commodity consumption implied the satisfaction of a need, the new economists go further: for them, every human decision is the evidence of a satisfying preference. They build economic models for crime, leisure, learning, fertility, discrimination and voting behavior. Marriage is no exception. Gary S. Becker, for instance, starts from the assumption of a sex-market in equilibrium, and hence derives formulas that describe the 'division of outputs between mates'. Others calculate the value added by the housewife to a TV dinner made by her unpaid activities in selecting, heating and serving it. Potentially, this line of thought would permit to argue that wage workers would be better off if they were to live as homebodies, that capital accumulation is what women have been doing unpaid at home. For Milton Friedman's pupils, *it is sex which offers a paradigm for the economics of what women do.*

A fourth mask is placed on shadow work by the majority of feminists writing on housework. They know that it is hard work. They fume because it is unpaid. Unlike most economists, they consider the wages lost huge, rather than trifling. Further, some of them believe that women's work is 'non-productive' and yet the main source of the "mystery of primitive accumulation", a contradiction that had baffled omniscient Marx. They add feminist sunshades to Marxist spectacles. They wed the house-wife to a wage-earning patriarch whose pay, rather than his penis, is the prime object of envy. They do not seem to have noticed that the redefinition of woman's nature after the French Revolution went hand in hand with that of man's. They are thus double blind both to the nineteenth century conspiracy of class enemies at the service of growth and to its reinforcement by the twentieth century war for the economic equality of the sexes they carry into each home. Abstract sex-roles in society at large rather than real pants in the home have become the issue of the domestic battle. The woman-oriented outlook of these feminists has helped them to publicize the degrading nature of unpaid work is now added to discrimination on the job, but their movement-specific commitment has compelled them to cloud the key issue: the fact that modern women are crippled by being compelled to labor that, in addition to being un-salaried in economic terms, is fruitless in terms of subsistence.

Recently, however, some new historians of women's work have penetrated beyond conventional categories and ap-proaches. They refuse to view their subject through hand-me-down professional glasses choosing rather to look from 'below the belt'. They study childbirth, breastfeeding, housecleaning, prostitution, rape, dirty laundry and speech, mother's love, child-hood, abortion, menopause. They have revealed how gyneco-logists, architects, druggists and colleagues in chairs of history reached into this disorderly grab bag to create symptoms and market novel therapies. Some of them unravel the home life of third world women in the new urban slums, and contrast it with the life in the *campo* or *kampung*. Others explore the 'labor of love' which was invented for women in neighborhoods, clinics and political parties.

The pathfinding innovators who dare to view industrial society from its shady and messy underside light up and dissect kinds of oppression heretofore hidden. What they then report does not fit the available -isms and -ologies. Not looking at the effects of industrialization from above, their findings turn out to be quite other than the pinnacles which managers describe, than the crevices which workers feel, than the principles which ideologues impose. And their eyes see differently than the ethno-anthropological explorers who are more accustomed through their training to view the Zande or to reconstruct a village priest's life in medieval Provence. Such unconventional research now violates a long-standing scholarly and political double taboo – the shadow which hides the Siamese twin nature of industrial work, and the prohibition to seek new terms to describe it.

Unlike the suffragettes of the social sciences, who seem obsessed by what enclosure has 'unjustly' denied them, the historians of female intimacy recognize that housework is *sui generis*. They detect the spread of a new shadow existence between 1780 and 1860, in different countries at a different rhythm. They report on a new life whose frustrations are not less painful when they are, occasionally, artfully guilded. They describe how this *sui generis* work was exported, together with wage labor, beyond the confines of Europe. And they observe that, wherever women became second best on the labor market, their work, when unpaid, was profoundly changed. Parallel with second-class wage work organized for women, first at the sewing machine, then at the typewriter and finally on the telephone, something new, the disestablished housewife came into being.

This transmogrification of housework is particularly obvious in the United States because it happened so abruptly. In 1810 the common productive unit in New England was still the rural household. Processing and preserving of food, candlemaking, soapmaking, spinning, weaving, shoemaking, quilting, rug-making, the keeping of small animals and gardens, all took place on domestic premises. Although money income might be obtained by the household through the sale of produce, and additional money be earned through occasional wages to its members, the United States household was overwhelmingly self-sufficient. Buying and selling, even when money did change hands, was often conducted on a barter basis. Women were as active in the creation of domestic self-sufficiency as were men. They brought home about the same salaries. They still were, *economically*, men's equals. In addition, they usually held the pursestrings. And further, they were as actively engaged in feeding, clothing and equipping the nation during the turn of the century. In 1810, in North America, twenty-four out of twenty-five yards of wool were of domestic origin. This picture had changed by 1830. Commercial farming had begun to re-place subsistence farms. The living wage had become common, and dependence on occasional wage work began to be seen as a sign of poverty. The woman, formerly the mistress of a house-hold that provided sustenance for the family, now became the guardian of a place where children stayed before they began to work, where the husband rested, and where his income was spent. Ann Douglas has called this transmogrification of women their 'disestablisment'. In fact, it strongly suggests the epoch's clerical aspirations and anxieties. Just as the clergyman of the time had been newly segregated in a strictly ecclesiastic realm, women were now both flattered and threatened to stick to their proper sphere where lip-service could be paid to the superiority of their functions. With their economic equality, women lost many of their legal privileges, among them the right to vote. They vanished from traditional trades, were replaced by male obstetricians in midwifery, and found the way into the new pro-fessions barred. Their economic disestablishment reflected society's commitment to the satisfaction of basic needs in the home by means of products created in wage labor that had moved away from the household. Deprived of subsistence, mar-ginal on the labor market, the frustrating task of the housewife became the organization of compulsory consumption. The exis-tence which is becoming typical of men and children in the 1980's was already well-known to a growing number of women in the 1850's.

The new historians of female sensitivity and mentality osten-sibly concentrate on women's work. But, in fact, they have given us the first coherent report written by trained historians who speak as losers in the war against subsistence. They provide

us a history of 'work' performed in the shadow of economic
searchlights, written by those who are compelled to do it. This
shadow, of course, blights much more than motherly or wifely
duties. It infallibly extends with progress and spreads with the
development of the economic sphere, reaching further into both
men's and women's lives to leave no one's day completely un-
clouded. The housewife will probably remain forever as the icon
of this shadow existence, just as the man in overalls will survive
the microprocessor as the icon of the 'industrial worker'. But to
make this other half of industrial existence into women's work,
tout court, would be the fifth and ultimate mystification. It would
forever besmirch the personal reality of women with a sex invented for economic control. For this reason, I propose 'shadow
work' to designate a social reality whose prototype is modern
housework. Add the rising number of unemployed to the increasing number of people kept on the job only to keep
them busy, and it becomes obvious that shadow work is by
far more common in our late industrial age than paid jobs.
By the end of the century, the productive worker will be the
exception.

Shadow work and wage labor came into existence together.
Both alienate equally, though they do so in profoundly different
ways. Bondage to shadow work was first achieved primarily
through economic sex-coupling. The nineteenth century bourgeois family made up of the wage earner and his dependents
replaced the subsistence-centered household. It tied the *femina
domestica* and a *vir laborans* in the thraldom of complementary
impotence typical for *homo economicus*. This crude model of bondage to shadow work could not suffice for economic expansion:
profits for capitalists are derived from compulsory consumers
just as the power of professionals and bureaucrats is derived
from disciplined clients. Both capitalists and commisars profit
more from shadow work than from wage labor. The sex-
coupling family provided them with a blueprint for more complex and more subtly disabling forms of bondage to shadow
work. This bondage today is effected essentially through social
agents empowered for diagnosis. Diagnosis literally means discrimination, knowing-apart. It is used today to designate the
act by which a profession defines you as its client. Whatever
allows a profession to impute a need for dependence on its

services will do quite well to impose the corresponding shadow work on the client. Medical scientists and pedagogues are typical examples of such disabling professions. They impose the shadow work of service consumption on their clients and get paid for it out of the clients' income, either directly or through taxed monies. In this fashion, the modern professionals who produce care push the pattern of the work-bonding modern family one step further: through wage labor, people in 'caring relationship' jobs now produce precisely those frustrating things which women in the nineteenth century family were originally compelled to do or make for no pay whatever. The creation of professionally supervised shadow work has become society's major business. Those paid to create shadow work are today's élite. As housework is only the most visible tip of shadow labor so the gynecological engineering of the housewife is only the most impudent cover for society-wide diagnostics. For example, the sixteen levels of relative degradation which define the classes of dropouts from the educational system assign disproportionate burdens of shadow work to society's lower and larger cohorts, and do so much more subtly than sex or race ever could have done.

The discovery of shadow work could well be, for the historian, as important as the discovery – a generation ago – of popular cultures and peasants as subjects of history. Then Karl Polanyi and the great Frenchmen around the *Annales* pioneered the study of the poor, of their ways of life, their sensibilities and world views. They brought the subsistence of the weak and illiterate into the realm of historical research. The study of women under the impact of industrialization can be understood as a beachhead into another no-man's-land of history: the forms of life that are typical only to industrial society yet remain invisible, as long as this society is studied under the assumptions about scarcity, desire, sex or work that it has secreted. The discovery of this shadow realm, which is distinct both from that of subsistent popular cultures and from that of political and social economy, will make those whom André Gorz calls 'post-proletarians' into subjects of history. And the historian will be able to see that the diagnostic procedure that first dis-established women by opposing them to men, in the meantime has dis-established everyone in multiple ways. In this perspective, the history of the industrial age is that of a radically new kind of discrimination.

This 'civil' war against popular cultures and vernacular values could never have succeeded unless those to be divested of subsistence had first accepted their enclosure into distinct spheres and thereby had been divided. The creation of the housewife bespeaks an unprecedented, a sexual apartheid. But it also illustrates the kind of consciousness in which desire could not but become mimetic. The many attempts to make this dividing line appear as a prolongation of traditional frontiers that have forever separated people from people, is as futile as the attempt to make industrial work appear as a prolongation of what people always did – both serve the same mystification. Both protect the taboo that covers the unexamined life of our age. People who insist on interpreting the current status of women as updated purdah must miss the point. Equally, those who view relegation to South African Homelands as a modern resettlement based on traditional attitudes toward distinct pigmentation totally miss the meaning of the color line. And anyone who sees the zek in the gulag primarily as a slave is blind to the motto that only a Hitler presumed to write large on the entrance to Auschwitz: "Arbeit macht frei". He will never understand a society in which the unpaid work of the Jew in the camp is exacted from him as his due contribution to his own extinction. Modern enclosure, apartheid, is never just cruel or just degrading, it has always a demonic dimension. Prose cannot do justice to a social organization set up to enlist people in their own destruction. To grasp its meaning we have to listen to the *Todesfuge* of Paul Celan, ". . . und sie schaufeln ein Grab in den Lüften . . . ein Grab in den Wolken, da liegt man nicht eng". The subtler forms of apartheid can blur our vision for the *mysterium iniquitatis* always inherent in them. Yesterday's fascism in Germany, or today's in South Africa manifest it.

Industrial society cannot forgo its victims. Nineteenth century women were enclosed, dis-established, they were damaged. Inevitably they had a corrupting influence on society at large. They provided that society with an object for *sentimental* compassion. Oppression always forces its victims to do society's dirty work. Our society forces its victims to become cooperative objects of oppression through care. Its condition for ordinary happiness is sentimental concern for others that ought to be helped, saved or liberated. This is the story that Nadine Gordimer told me, not about women, not about pupils, patients or inmates, but about blacks. She told it to me with "the deceptive commonplace that people, accustomed to police harassment, use before the uninitiated", an attitude that she attributes to her main character, Burger's daughter. For her there is no ordinary happiness, because she is ill. The illness that she describes is the loss of that sentimentalism on which ordinary happiness today depends.

Ann Douglas, the American, has well described this sentimentalism. It is a complex phenomenon that in industrial societies is the substratum of ideologies and religions. It asserts that the values that an industrial society's activities deny are precisely those that it cherishes. It asserts that the values now attributed to subsistence – subsistence which economic growth inevitably destroys – are precisely those for the sake of which growth must continue. It transmogrifies subsistence into the economy's shadow. Sentimentalism succeeds in dealing with the apartheid, implicit in the opposition between production and consumption, by manipulating nostalgia for subsistence. And this 'subsistence' to which nostalgia aspires, turns out to be the economy's shadow which is the converse of the vernacular domain. The sentimental glorification of the victims of apartheid: women, patients, blacks, illiterates, the underdeveloped, addicts, the underdog, the proletariat, provides a way to solemnly protest a power to which one has already capitulated. This sentimentalism is a dishonesty for which there is no known substitute in a society that has ravished its own environment for subsistence. Such a society depends on ever new diagnoses of those for whom it must care. And this paternalistic dishonesty enables the representatives of the oppressed to seek power for ever new oppression.

ENERGY AND EQUITY

by Ivan Illich

El socialismo puede llegar solo en bicicleta.

José Antonio Viera-Gallo, Assistant Secretary of Justice in the government of Salvador Allende

Illich italicized these paragraphs prefacing *Energy & Equity* when he republished it in *Towards a History of Needs* (Berkeley: Heyday Books).

This text was first published in Le Monde *in early 1973. Over lunch in Paris the venerable editor of that daily, as he accepted my manuscript, recommended just one change. He felt that a term as little known and as technical as "energy crisis" had no place in the opening sentence of an article that he would be running on page 1. As I now reread the text, I am struck by the speed with which language and issues have shifted in less than five years. But I am equally struck by the slow yet steady pace at which the radical alternative to industrial society – namely, low-energy, convivial modernity – has gained defenders.*

In this essay I argue that under some circumstances, a technology incorporates the values of the society for which it was invented to such a degree that these values become dominant in every society which applies that technology. The material structure of production devices can thus irremediably incorporate class prejudice. High-energy technology, at least as applied to traffic, provides a clear example. Obviously, this thesis undermines the legitimacy of those professionals who monopolize the operation of such technologies. It is particularly irksome to those individuals within the professions who seek to served the public by using the rhetoric of class struggle with the aim of replacing the "capitalists" who now control institutional policy by professional peers and laymen who accept professional standards. Mainly under the influence of such "radical" professionals, this thesis has, in only five years, changed from an oddity into a heresy that has provoked a barrage of abuse.

The distinction proposed here, however, is not new. I oppose tools that can be applied in the generation of use-values to others that cannot be used except in the production of commodities. This distinction has recently been re-emphasized by a great variety of social critics. The insistence on the need for a balance between convivial and industrial tools is, in fact, the common distinctive element in an emerging consensus among groups engaged in radical politics. A superb guide to the bibliography in this field has been published in Radical Technology *(London and New York, 1976) by the editors of* Undercurrents. *I have transferred my own files on the theme to Valentina Borremans, who is now working on a librarians' guide to reference materials on use-value-oriented modern tools, scheduled for publication in 1978. (Preliminary drafts of individual chapters of this guide can be obtained by writing to Valentina Borremans, APDO 479, Cuernavaca, Mexico.) The specific argument on socially critical energy thresholds in transportation that I pursue in this essay has been elaborated and documented by two colleagues, Jean-Pierre Dupuy and Jean Robert, in their two jointly written books,* La Trahison de l'opulence *(Paris, 1976) and* Les Chronophages *(Paris, 1978).*

Ivan Illich: Toward a History of Needs. Pantheon, New York, 1978

The Energy Crisis

It has recently become fashionable to insist on an impending energy crisis. This euphemistic term conceals a contradiction and consecrates an illusion. It masks the contradiction implicit in the joint pursuit of equity and industrial growth. It safeguards the illusion that machine power can indefinitely take the place of manpower. To resolve this contradiction and dispel this illusion, it is urgent to clarify the reality that the language of crisis obscures: high quanta of energy degrade social relations just as inevitably as they destroy the physical milieu.

The advocates of an energy crisis believe in and continue to propagate a peculiar vision of man. According to this notion, man is born into perpetual dependence on slaves which he must painfully learn to master. If he does not employ prisoners, then he needs machines to do most of his work. According to this doctrine, the well-being of a society can be measured by the number of years its members have gone to school and by the number of energy slaves they have thereby learned to command. This belief is common to the conflicting economic ideologies now in vogue. It is threatened by the obvious inequity, harriedness, and impotence that appear everywhere once the voracious hordes of energy slaves outnumber people by a certain proportion. The energy crisis focuses concern on the scarcity of fodder for these slaves. I prefer to ask whether free men need them.

The energy policies adopted during the current decade will determine the range and character of social relationships a society will be able to enjoy by the year 2000. A low-energy policy allows for a wide choice of life-styles and cultures. If, on the other hand, a society opts for high energy consumption, its social relations must be dictated by technocracy and will be equally degrading whether labeled capitalist or socialist.

At this moment, most societies – especially the poor ones – are still free to set their energy policies by any of three guidelines. Well-being can be identified with high amounts of per capita energy use, with high efficiency of energy transformation, or with the least possible use of mechanical energy by the most powerful members of society. The first approach would stress tight management of scarce and destructive fuels on behalf of industry, whereas the second would emphasize the retooling of industry in the interest of thermodynamic thrift. These first two attitudes necessarily imply huge public expenditures and increased social control; both rationalize the emergence of a computerized Leviathan, and both are at present widely discussed.

The possibility of a third option is barely noticed. While people have begun to accept ecological limits on maximum per capita energy use as a condition for physical survival, they do not yet think about the use of minimum feasible power as the foundation of any of various social orders that would be both modern and desirable. Yet only a ceiling on energy use can lead to social relations that are characterized by high levels of equity. The one option that is at present neglected is the only choice within the reach of all nations. It is also the only strategy by which a political process can be used to set limits on the power of even the most motorized bureaucrat. Participatory democracy postulates low-energy technology. Only participatory democracy creates the conditions for rational technology.

What is generally overlooked is that equity and energy can grow concurrently only to a point. Below a threshold of per capita wattage, motors improve the conditions for social progress. Above this threshold, energy grows at the expense of equity. Further energy affluence then means decreased distribution of control over that energy.

The widespread belief that clean and abundant energy is the panacea for social ills is due to a political fallacy, according to which equity and energy consumption can be indefinitely correlated, at least under some ideal political conditions. Laboring under this illusion, we tend to discount any social limit on the growth of energy consumption. But if ecologists are right to assert that nonmetabolic power pollutes, it is in fact just as inevitable that, beyond a certain threshold, mechanical power corrupts. The threshold of social disintegration by high energy quanta is independent from the threshold at which energy conversion produces physical destruction. Expressed in horsepower, it is undoubtedly lower. This is the fact which must be theoretically recognized before a political issue can be made of the per capita wattage to which a society will limit its members.

Even if nonpolluting power were feasible and abundant, the use of energy on a massive scale acts on society like a drug that is physically harmless but psychically enslaving. A community can choose between Methadone and 'cold turkey' – between maintaining its addiction to alien energy and kicking it in painful cramps – but no society can have a population that is hooked on progressively larger numbers of energy slaves and whose members are also autonomously active.

In previous discussions, I have shown that, beyond a certain level of per capita GNP, the cost of social control must rise faster than total output and become the major institutional activity within an economy. Therapy administered by educators, psychiatrists, and social workers must converge with the designs of planners, managers, and salesmen, and complement the services of security agencies, the military, and the police. I now want to indicate one reason why increased affluence requires increased control over people. I argue that beyond a certain median per capita energy level, the political system and cultural context of any society must decay. Once the critical quantum of per capita energy is surpassed, education for the abstract goals of a bureaucracy must supplant the legal guarantees of personal and concrete initiative. This quantum is the limit of social order.

I will argue here that technocracy must prevail as soon as the ratio of mechanical power to metabolic energy oversteps a definite, identifiable threshold. The order of magnitude within which this threshold lies is largely independent of the level of technology applied, yet its very existence has slipped into the blind-spot of social imagination in both rich and medium-rich countries. Both the United States and Mexico have passed the critical divide. In both countries, further energy inputs increase inequality, inefficiency, and personal impotence. Although one country has a per capita income of $500 and the other, one of nearly $5,000, huge vested interest in an industrial infrastructure prods both of them to further escalate the use of energy. As a result, both North American and Mexican ideologues put the label of 'energy crisis' on their frustration, and both countries are blinded to the fact that the threat of social breakdown is due neither to a shortage of fuel nor to the wasteful, polluting, and irrational use of available wattage, but to the attempt of industries to gorge society with energy quanta that inevitably degrade, deprive, and frustrate most people.

A people can be just as dangerously overpowered by the wattage of its tools as by the caloric content of its foods, but it is much harder to confess to a national overindulgence in wattage than to a sickening diet. The per capita wattage that is critical for social well-being lies within an order of magnitude which is far above the horsepower known to four-fifths of humanity and far below the power commanded by any Volkswagen driver. It eludes the underconsumer and the overconsumer alike. Neither is willing to face the facts. For the primitive, the elimination of slavery and drudgery depends on the introduction of appropriate modern technology, and for the rich, the avoidance of an even more horrible degradation depends on the effective recognition of a threshold in energy consumption beyond which technical processes begin to dictate social relations. Calories are both biologically and socially healthy only as long as they stay within the narrow range that separates enough from too much.

The so-called energy crisis is, then, a politically ambiguous issue. Public interest in the quantity of power and in the distribution of controls over the use of energy can lead in two opposite directions. On the one hand, questions can be posed that would open the way to political reconstruction by unblocking the search for a postindustrial, labor-intensive, low-energy and high-equity economy. On the other hand, hysterical concern with machine fodder can reinforce the present escalation of capital-intensive institutional growth, and carry us past the last turnoff from a hyperindustrial Armageddon. Political reconstruction presupposes the recognition of the fact that there exist critical per capita quanta beyond which energy can no longer be controlled by political process. A universal social straitjacket will be the inevitable outcome of ecological restraints on total energy use imposed by industrial-minded planners bent on keeping industrial production at some hypothetical maximum.

Rich countries like the United States, Japan, or France might never reach the point of choking on their own waste, but only because their societies will have already collapsed into a sociocultural energy coma. Countries like India, Burma, and, for another short while at least, China are in the inverse position of being still muscle-powered enough to stop short of an energy stroke. They could choose, right now, to stay within those limits to which the rich will be forced back through a total loss of their freedoms.

The choice of a minimum-energy economy compels the poor to abandon fantastical expectations and the rich to recognize their vested interest as a ghastly liability. Both must reject the fatal image of man the slaveholder currently promoted by an ideologically stimulated hunger for more energy. In countries that were made affluent by industrial development, the energy crisis serves as a pretext for raising the taxes that will be needed to substitute new, more 'rational', and socially more deadly industrial processes for those that have been rendered obsolete by inefficient overexpansion. For the leaders of people who are not yet dominated by the same process of industrialization, the energy crisis serves as a historical imperative to centralize production, pollution, and their control in a last-ditch effort to catch up with the more highly powered. By exporting their crisis and by preaching the new gospel of puritan energy worship, the rich do even more damage to the poor than they did by selling them the products of now outdated factories. As soon as a poor country accepts the doctrine that more energy more carefully managed will always yield more goods for more people, that country locks itself into the cage of enslavement to maximum industrial outputs. Inevitably the poor lose the option for rational technology when they choose to modernize their poverty by increasing their dependence on energy. Inevitably the poor deny themselves the possibility of liberating technology and participatory politics when, together with maximum feasible energy use, they accept maximum feasible social control.

The energy crisis cannot be overwhelmed by more energy inputs. It can only be dissolved, along with the illusion that well-being depends on the number of energy slaves a man has at his command. For this purpose, it is necessary to identify the thresholds beyond which energy corrupts, and to do so by a political process that associates the community in the search for limits. Because this kind of research runs counter to that now done by experts and for institutions, I shall continue to call it counterfoil research. It has three steps. First, the need for limits on the per capita use of energy must be theoretically recognized as a social imperative. Then, the range must be located wherein the critical magnitude might be found. Finally, each community has to identify the levels of inequity, harrying, and operant conditioning that its members are willing to accept in exchange for the satisfaction that comes of idolizing powerful devices and joining in rituals directed by the professionals who control their operation.

The need for political research on socially optimal energy quanta can be clearly and concisely illustrated by an examination of modern traffic. The United States puts between 25 and 45 per cent of its total energy (depending upon how one calculates this) into vehicles: to make them, run them, and clear a right of way for them when they roll, when they fly, and when they park. Most of this energy is to move people who have been strapped into place. For the sole purpose of transporting people, 250 million Americans allocate more fuel than is used by 1.3 billion Chinese and Indians for all purposes. Almost all of this fuel is burned in a rain-dance of time-consuming acceleration. Poor countries spend less energy per person, but the percentage of total energy devoted to traffic in Mexico or in Peru is probably greater than in the United States, and it benefits a smaller percentage of the population. The size of this enterprise makes it both easy and significant to demonstrate the existence of socially critical energy quanta by the example of personal mobility.

In traffic, energy used over a specific period of time (power) translates into speed. In this case, the critical quantum will appear as a speed limit. Wherever this limit has been passed, the basic pattern of social degradation by high energy quanta has emerged. Once some public utility went faster than 15 mph, equity declined and the scarcity of both time and space increased. Motorized transportation monopolized traffic and blocked self-powered transit. In every Western country, passenger mileage on all types of conveyance increased by a factor of a hundred within fifty years of building the first railroad. When the ratio of their respective power outputs passed beyond a certain value, mechanical transformers of mineral fuels excluded people from the use of their metabolic energy and forced them to become captive consumers of conveyance. This effect of speed on the autonomy of people is only marginally affected by the technological characteristics of the motorized vehicles employed or by the persons or entities who hold the legal titles to airlines, buses, railroads, or cars. High speed is the critical factor which makes transportation socially destructive. A true choice among practical policies and of desirable social relations is possible only where speed is restrained. Participatory democracy demands low-energy technology, and free people must travel the road to productive social relations at the speed of a bicycle.

The Industrialization of Traffic

The discussion of how energy is used to move people requires a formal distinction between transport and transit as the two components of traffic. By *traffic* I mean any movement of people from one place to another when they are outside their homes. By *transit* I mean those movements that put human metabolic energy to use, and by *transport*, that mode of movement which relies on other sources of energy. These energy sources will henceforth be mostly motors, since animals compete fiercely with men for their food in an overpopulated world, unless they are thistle eaters like donkeys and camels.

As soon as people become tributaries of transport, not just when they travel for several days, but also on their daily trips, the contradictions between social justice and motorized power, between effective movement and higher speed, between personal freedom and engineered routing, become poignantly clear. Enforced dependence on auto-mobile machines then denies a community of self-propelled people just those values supposedly procured by improved transportation.

People move well on their feet. This primitive means of getting around will, on closer analysis, appear quite effective when compared with the lot of people in modern cities or on industrialized farms. It will appear particularly attractive once it has been understood that modern Americans walk, on the average, as many miles as their ancestors – most of them through tunnels, corridors, parking lots, and stores.

People on their feet are more or less equal. People solely dependent on their feet move on the spur of the moment, at three to four miles per hour, in any direction and to any place from which they are not legally or physically barred. An improvement on this native degree of mobility by new transport technology should be expected to safeguard these values and to add some new ones, such as greater range, time economies, comfort, or more opportunities for the disabled. So far this is not what has happened. Instead, the growth of the transportation industry has everywhere had the reverse effect. From the moment its machines could put more than a certain horsepower behind any one passenger, this industry has reduced equality among men, restricted their mobility to a system of industrially defined routes, and created time scarcity of unprecedented severity. As the speed of their vehicles crosses a threshold, citizens become transportation consumers on the daily loop that brings them back to their home, a circuit which the United States Department of Commerce calls a 'trip' as opposed to the 'travel' for which Americans leave home equipped with a toothbrush.

More energy fed into the transportation system means that more people move faster over a greater range in the course of every day. Everybody's daily radius expands at the expense of being able to drop in on an acquaintance or walk through the park on the way to work. Extremes of privilege are created at the cost of universal enslavement. An elite packs unlimited distance into a lifetime of pampered travel, while the majority spend a bigger slice of their existence on unwanted trips. The few mount their magic carpets to travel between distant points that their ephemeral presence renders both scarce and seductive, while the many are compelled to trip farther and faster and to spend more time preparing for and recovering from their trips.

In the United States, four-fifths of all man-hours on the road are those of commuters and shoppers who hardly ever get into a plane, while four-fifths of the mileage flown to conventions and resorts is covered year after year by the same 1.5 per cent of the population, usually those who are either well-to-do or professionally trained to do good. The speedier the vehicle, the larger the subsidy it gets from regressive taxation. Barely 0.2 per cent of the entire United States population can engage in self-chosen air travel more than once a year, and few other countries can support a jet set which is that large.

The captive tripper and the reckless traveler become equally dependent on transport. Neither can do without it. Occasional spurts to Acapulco or to a party congress dupe the ordinary passenger into believing that he has made it into the shrunk world of the powerfully rushed. The occasional chance to spend a few hours strapped into a high-powered seat makes him an accomplice in the distortion of human space, and prompts him to consent to the design of his country's geography around vehicles rather than around people. Man has evolved physically and culturally together with his cosmic niche. What for animals is their environment he has learned to make into his home. His self-consciousness requires as its complement a life-space and a life-time integrated by the pace at which he moves. If that relationship is determined by the velocity of vehicles rather than by the movement of people, man the architect is reduced to the status of a mere commuter.

The model American male devotes more than 1,600 hours a year to his car. He sits in it while it goes and while it stands idling. He parks it and searches for it. He earns the money to put down on it and to meet the monthly installments. He works to pay for gasoline, tolls, insurance, taxes, and tickets. He spends four of his sixteen waking hours on the road or gathering his resources for it. And this figure does not take into account the time consumed by other activities dictated by transport: time spent in hospitals, traffic courts, and garages; time spent watching automobile commercials or attending consumer education meetings to improve the quality of the next buy. The model American puts in 1,600 hours to get 7,500 miles: less than five miles per hour. In countries deprived of a transportation industry, people manage to do the same, walking wherever they want to go, and they allocate only 3 to 8 per cent of their society's time budget to traffic instead of 28 per cent. What distinguishes the traffic in rich countries from the traffic in poor countries is not more mileage per hour of life-time for the majority, but more hours of compulsory consumption of high doses of energy, packaged and unequally distributed by the transportation industry.

Speed-stunned Imagination

Past a certain threshold of energy consumption, the transportation industry dictates the configuration of social space. Motorways expand, driving wedges between neighbors and removing fields beyond the distance a farmer can walk. Ambulances take clinics beyond the few miles a sick child can be carried. The doctor will no longer come to the house, because vehicles have made the hospital into the right place to be sick. Once heavy trucks reach a village high in the Andes, part of the local market disappears. Later, when the high school arrives at the plaza along with the paved highway, more and more of the young people move to the city, until not one family is left which does not long for a reunion with someone hundreds of miles away, down on the coast.

Equal speeds have equally distorting effects on the perception of space, time, and personal potency in rich and in poor countries, however different the surface appearances might be. Everywhere, the transportation industry shapes a new kind of man to fit the new geography and the new schedules of its making. The major difference between Guatemala and Kansas is that in Central America some provinces are still exempt from all contact with vehicles and are, therefore, still not degraded by their dependence on them.

The product of the transportation industry is the habitual passenger. He has been boosted out of the world in which people still move on their own, and he has lost the sense that he stands at the center of his world. The habitual passenger is conscious of the exasperating time scarcity that results from daily recourse to the cars, trains, buses, subways, and elevators that force him to cover an average of twenty miles each day, frequently crisscrossing his path within a radius of less than five miles. He has been lifted off his feet. No matter if he goes by subway or jet plane, he feels slower and poorer than someone else and resents the shortcuts taken by the privileged few who can escape the frustrations of traffic. If he is cramped by the timetable of his commuter train, he dreams of a car. If he drives, exhausted by the rush hour, he envies the speed capitalist who drives against the traffic. If he must pay for his car out of his own pocket, he knows full well that the commanders of corporate fleets send the fuel bill to the company and write off the rented car as a business expense. The habitual passenger is caught at the wrong end of growing inequality, time scarcity, and personal impotence, but he can see no way out of this bind except to demand more of the same: more traffic by transport. He stands in wait for technical changes in the design of vehicles, roads, and schedules; or else he expects a revolution to produce mass rapid transport under public control. In neither case does he calculate the price of being hauled into a better future. He forgets that he is the one who will pay the bill, either in fares or in taxes. He overlooks the hidden costs of replacing private cars with equally rapid public transport.

The habitual passenger cannot grasp the folly of traffic based overwhelmingly on transport. His inherited perceptions of space and time and of personal pace have been industrially deformed. He has lost the power to conceive of himself outside the passenger role. Addicted to being carried along, he has lost control over the physical, social, and psychic powers that reside in man's feet. The passenger has come to identify territory with the untouchable landscape through which he is rushed. He has become impotent to establish his domain, mark it with his imprint, and assert his sovereignty over it. He has lost confidence in his power to admit others into his presence and to share space consciously with them. He can no longer face the remote by himself. Left on his own, he feels immobile.

The habitual passenger must adopt a new set of beliefs and expectations if he is to feel secure in the strange world where both liaisons and loneliness are products of conveyance. To 'gather' for him means to be brought together by vehicles. He comes to believe that political power grows out of the capacity of a transportation system, and in its absence is the result of access to the television screen. He takes freedom of movement to be the same as one's claim on propulsion. He believes that the level of democratic process correlates to the power of transportation and communications systems. He has lost faith in the political power of the feet and of the tongue. As a result, what he wants is not more liberty as a citizen but better service as a client. He does not insist on his freedom to move and to speak to people but on his claim to be shipped and to be informed by media. He wants a better product rather than freedom from servitude to it. It is vital that he come to see that the acceleration he demands is self-defeating, and that it must result in a further decline of equity, leisure, and autonomy.

Net Transfer of Lifetime

Unchecked speed is expensive, and progressively fewer can afford it. Each increment in the velocity of a vehicle results in an increase in the cost of propulsion and track construction and – most dramatically – in the space the vehicle devours while it is on the move. Past a certain threshold of energy consumption for the fastest passenger, a worldwide class structure of speed capitalists is created. The exchange-value of time becomes dominant, and this is reflected in language: time is spent, saved, invested, wasted, and employed. As societies put price tags on time, equity and vehicular speed correlate inversely.

High speed capitalizes a few people's time at an enormous rate but, paradoxically, it does this at a high cost in time for all. In Bombay, only a very few people own cars. They can reach a provincial capital in one morning and make the trip once a week. Two generations ago, this would have been a week-long trek once a year. They now spend more time on more trips. But these same few also disrupt, with their cars, the traffic flow of thousands of bicycles and pedicabs that move through downtown Bombay at a rate of effective locomotion that is still superior to that of downtown Paris, London, or New York. The compounded, transport-related time expenditure within a society grows much faster than the time economies made by a few people on their speedy excursions. Traffic grows indefinitely with the availability of high-speed transports. Beyond a critical threshold, the output of the industrial complex established to move people costs a society more time than it saves. The marginal utility of an increment in the speed of a small number of people has for its price the growing marginal disutility of this acceleration for the great majority.

Beyond a critical speed, no one can save time without forcing another to lose it. The man who claims a seat in a faster vehicle insists that his time is worth more than that of the passenger in a slower one. Beyond a certain velocity, passengers become consumers of other people's time, and accelerating vehicles become the means for effecting a net transfer of life-time. The degree of transfer is measured in quanta of speed. This time grab despoils those who are left behind, and since they are the majority, it raises ethical issues of a more general nature than the lottery that assigns kidney dialysis or organ transplants.

Beyond a certain speed, motorized vehicles create remoteness which they alone can shrink. They create distances for all and shrink them for only a few. A new dirt road through the wilderness brings the city within view, but not within reach, of most Brazilian subsistence farmers. The new expressway expands Chicago, but it sucks those who are well-wheeled away from a downtown that decays into a ghetto.

Contrary to what is often claimed, man's speed remained unchanged from the Age of Cyrus to the Age of Steam. News did not travel more than a hundred miles per day, no matter how the message was carried. Neither the Inca's runners nor the Venetian galley, the Persian horseman, or the mail coach on regular runs under Louis XIV broke the barrier. Soldiers, explorers, merchants, and pilgrims moved at twenty miles per day. In Valéry's words, Napoleon still had to move at Caesar's slowness: *Napoléon va à la même lenteur que César.* The emperor knew that "public prosperity is measured by the income of the coaches": *On mesure la prospérité publique aux comptes des diligences,* but he could barely speed them up. Paris – Toulouse had required about 200 hours in Roman times, and the scheduled stagecoach still took 158 hours in 1740, before the opening of the new Royal Roads. Only the nineteenth century accelerated man. By 1830, the trip had been reduced to 110 hours, but at a new cost. In the same year, 4,150 stagecoaches overturned in France, causing more than a thousand deaths. Then the railroad brought a sudden change. By 1855, Napoleon III claimed to have hit 96 kilometers per hour on the train somewhere between Paris and Marseilles. Within one generation, the average distance traveled each year per Frenchman increased one hundred and thirty times, and Britain's railroad network reached its greatest expansion. Passenger trains attained their optimum cost calculated in terms of time spent for their maintenance and use.

With further acceleration, transportation began to dominate traffic, and speed began to erect a hierarchy of destinations. By now, each set of destinations corresponds to a specific level of speed and defines a certain passenger class. Each circuit of terminal points degrades those pegged at a lower number of miles per hour. Those who must get around on their own power have been redefined as underdeveloped outsiders. Tell me how fast you go and I'll tell you who you are. If you can corner the taxes that fuel the Concorde, you are certainly at the top.

Over the last two generations, the vehicle has become the sign of career achievement, just as the school has become the sign of starting advantage. At each new level, the concentration of power must produce its own kind of rationale. So, for example, the reason that is usually given for spending public money to make a man travel more miles in less time each year is the still greater investment that was made to keep him more years in school. His putative value as a capital-intensive production tool sets the rate at which he is being shipped. Other ideological labels besides 'a good education' are just as useful for opening the cabin door to luxuries paid for by others. If the Thought of Chairman Mao must now be rushed around China by jet, this can only mean that two classes are needed to fuel what his revolution has become, one of them living in the geography of the masses and the other in the geography of the cadres. The suppression of intermediary levels of speed in the People's Republic has certainly made the concentration of power more efficient and rational, but it also underscores the new difference in value between the time of the bullock driver and the time of the jet-driven. Acceleration inevitably concentrates horsepower under the seats of a few and compounds the increasing time lack of most commuters with the further sense that they are lagging behind.

The need for unequal privilege in an industrial society is generally advocated by means of an argument with two sides. The hypocrisy of this argument is clearly betrayed by acceleration. Privilege is accepted as the necessary precondition for improving the lot of a growing total population, or it is advertised as the instrument for raising the standards of a deprived minority. In the long run, accelerating transportation does neither. It only creates a universal demand for motorized conveyance and puts previously unimaginable distances between the various layers of privilege. Beyond a certain point, more energy means less equity.

The Ineffectiveness of Acceleration

It should not be overlooked that top speeds for a few exact a different price than high speeds for all. Social classification by levels of speed enforces a net transfer of power: the poor work and pay to get left behind. But if the middle classes of a speed society may be tempted to ignore discrimination, they should not neglect the rising marginal disutilities of transportation and their own loss of leisure. High speeds for all mean that everybody has less time for himself as the whole society spends a growing slice of its time budget on moving people. Vehicles running over the critical speed not only tend to impose inequality, they also inevitably establish a self-serving industry that hides an inefficient system of locomotion under apparent technological sophistication. I will argue that a speed limit is not only necessary to safeguard equity; it is equally a condition for increasing the total distance traveled within a society, while simultaneously decreasing the sum total of life-time that transportation claims.

There is little research available on the impact of vehicles on the twenty-four-hour time budget of individuals and societies. From transportation studies, we get statistics on the cost of time per mile, on the value of time measured in dollars or in length of trips. But these statistics tell us nothing about the hidden costs of transportation: about how traffic nibbles away at lifetime, about how vehicles devour space, about the multiplication of trips made necessary by the existence of vehicles, or about the time spent directly and indirectly preparing for locomotion. Further, there is no available measure of the even more deeply buried costs of transport, such as higher rent to live in areas convenient to the flow of traffic, or the cost of protecting these areas from the noise, pollution, and danger to life and limb that vehicles create. The lack of an account of expenditures from the social time budget should not lead us to believe, however, that such an accounting is impossible, nor should it prevent our drawing conclusions from the little that we do know.

From our limited information it appears that everywhere in the world, after some vehicle broke the speed barrier of 15 mph, time scarcity related to traffic began to grow. After industry had reached this threshold of per capita output, transport made of man a new kind of waif: a being constantly absent from a destination he cannot reach on his own but must attain within the day. By now, people work a substantial part of every day to earn the money without which they could not even get to work. The time a society spends on transportation grows in proportion to the speed of its fastest public conveyance. Japan now leads the United States in both areas. Life-time gets cluttered up with activities generated by traffic as soon as vehicles crash through the barrier that guards people from dislocation and space from distortion.

Whether the vehicle that speeds along the public freeway is owned by the state or by an individual has little to do with the time scarcity and over-programming that rise with every increment in speed. Buses use one-third of the fuel that cars burn to carry one man over a given distance. Commuter trains are up to ten times more efficient than cars. Both could become even more efficient and less polluting. If publicly owned and rationally managed, they could be so scheduled and routed that the privileges they now provide under private ownership and incompetent organization would be considerably cut. But as long as any system of vehicles imposes itself on the public by top speeds that are not under political control, the public is left to choose between spending more time to pay for more people to be carried from station to station, and paying less taxes so that even fewer people can travel in much less time much farther than others. The order of magnitude of the top speed that is permitted within a transportation system determines the slice of its time budget that an entire society spends on traffic.

The Radical Monopoly of Industry

A desirable ceiling on the velocity of movement cannot be usefully discussed without returning to the distinction between self-powered *transit* and motorized *transport*, and comparing the contribution each component makes relative to the total loco-motion of people, which I have called *traffic*.

Transport stands for the capital-intensive mode of traffic, and transit indicates the labor-intensive mode. Transport is the product of an industry whose clients are passengers. It is an industrial commodity and therefore scarce by definition. Improvement of transport always takes place under conditions of scarcity that become more severe as the speed – and with it the cost – of the service increases. Conflict about insufficient transport tends to take the form of a zero-sum game where one wins only if another loses. At best, such a conflict allows for the optimum in the Prisoner's Dilemma: by cooperating with their jailer, both prisoners get off with less time in the cell.

Transit is not the product of an industry but the independent enterprise of transients. It has use-value by definition but need not have any exchange-value. The ability to engage in transit is native to man and more or less equally distributed among healthy people of the same age. The exercise of this ability can be restricted by depriving some class of people of the right to take a straight route, or because a population lacks shoes or pavements. Conflict about unsatisfactory transit conditions tends to take, therefore, the form of a non-zero-sum game in which everyone comes out ahead – not only the people who get the right to walk through a formerly walled property, but also those who live along the road.

Total traffic is the result of two profoundly distinct modes of production. These can reinforce each other harmoniously only as long as the autonomous outputs are protected against the encroachment of the industrial product.

The harm done by contemporary traffic is due to the monopoly of transport. The allure of speed has deceived the passenger into accepting the promises made by an industry that produces capital-intensive traffic. He is convinced that high-speed vehicles have allowed him to progress beyond the limited autonomy he enjoyed when moving under his own power. He has allowed planned transport to predominate over the alternative of labor-intensive transit. Destruction of the physical environment is the least noxious effect of this concession. The far more bitter results are the multiplication of psychic frustration, the growing disutilities of continued production, and subjection to an inequitable transfer of power – all of which are manifestations of a distorted relationship between life-time and life-space. The passenger who agrees to live in a world monopolized by transport becomes a harassed, overburdened consumer of distances whose shape and length he can no longer control.

Every society that imposes compulsory speed submerges transit to the profit of transport. Wherever not only privilege but also elementary necessities are denied to those who do not use high-speed conveyances, an involuntary acceleration of personal rhythms is imposed. Industry dominates traffic as soon as daily life comes to depend on motorized trips.

This profound control of the transportation industry over natural mobility constitutes a monopoly much more pervasive than either the commercial monopoly Ford might win over the automobile market, or the political monopoly car manufacturers might wield against the development of trains and buses. Because of its hidden, entrenched, and structuring nature, I call this a *radical monopoly*. Any industry exercises this kind of deep-seated monopoly when it becomes the dominant means of satisfying needs that formerly occasioned a personal response. The compulsory consumption of a high-powered commodity (motorized transport) restricts the conditions for enjoying an abundant use-value (the innate capacity for transit). Traffic serves here as the paradigm of a general economic law: *Any industrial product that comes in per capita quanta beyond a given intensity exercises a radical monopoly over the satisfaction of a need.* Beyond some point, compulsory schooling destroys the environment for learning, medical delivery systems dry up the non-therapeutic sources of health, and transportation smothers traffic.

Radical monopoly is first established by a rearrangement of society for the benefit of those who have access to the larger quanta, then it is enforced by compelling all to consume the minimum quantum in which the output is currently produced. Compulsory consumption will take on a different appearance in industrial branches where information dominates, such as education or medicine, than it will in those branches where quanta can be measured in British thermal units, such as housing, clothing, or transport. The industrial packaging of values will reach critical intensity at different points with different products, but for each major class of outputs, the threshold occurs within an order of magnitude that is theoretically identifiable. The fact that it is possible theoretically to determine the range of speed within which transportation develops a radical monopoly over traffic does not mean that it is possible theoretically to determine just how much of such a monopoly any given society will tolerate. The fact that it is possible to identify a level of compulsory instruction at which learning by seeing and doing declines does not enable the theorist to identify the specific pedagogical limits to the division of labor that a culture will tolerate. Only recourse to juridical and, above all, to political process can lead to the specific, though provisional, measures by which speed or compulsory education will actually be limited in a given society. The magnitude of voluntary limits is a matter of politics; the encroachment of radical monopoly can be pinpointed by social analysis.

A branch of industry does not impose a radical monopoly on a whole society by the simple fact that it produces scarce products, or by driving competing industries off the market, but rather by virtue of its acquired ability to create and shape the need which it alone can satisfy.

Shoes are scarce all over Latin America, and many people never wear them. They walk on the bare soles of their feet, or wear the world's widest variety of excellent sandals, supplied by a range of artisans. Their transit is in no way restricted by their lack of shoes. But in some countries of South America people are compelled to be shod ever since access to schools, jobs, and public services was denied to the barefoot. Teachers or party officials define the lack of shoes as a sign of indifference toward 'progress.' Without any intentional conspiracy between the promoters of national development and the shoe industry, the barefoot in these countries are now barred from any office.

Schools, like shoes, have been scarce at all times. But it was never the small number of privileged pupils that turned the school into an obstacle for learning. Only when laws were enacted to make schools both compulsory and free did the educator assume the power to deny learning opportunities on the job to the underconsumer of educational therapies. Only when school attendance had become obligatory did it become feasible to impose on all a progressively more complex artificial environment into which the unschooled and unprogrammed do not fit.

The potential of a radical monopoly is unmistakable in the case of traffic. Imagine what would happen if the transportation industry could somehow distribute its output more adequately: a traffic utopia of free *rapid* transportation for all would inevitably lead to a further expansion of traffic's domain over human life. What would such a utopia look like? Traffic would be organized exclusively around public transportation systems. It would be financed by a progressive tax calculated on income and on the proximity of one's residence to the next terminal and to the job. It would be designed so that everybody could occupy any seat on a first-come, first-served basis: the doctor, the vacationer, and the president would not be assigned any priority of person. In this fool's paradise, all passengers would be equal, but they would be just as equally captive consumers of transport. Each citizen of a motorized utopia would be equally deprived of the use of his feet and equally drafted into the servitude of proliferating networks of transportation.

Certain would-be miracle makers disguised as architects offer a specious escape from the paradox of speed. By their standards, acceleration imposes inequities, time loss, and controlled schedules only because people do not yet live in those patterns and orbits into which vehicles can best place them. These futuristic architects would house and occupy people in self-sufficient units of towers interconnected by tracks for high-speed capsules. Soleri, Doxiadis, or Fuller would solve the problem created by high-speed transport by identifying the entire human habitat with the problem. Rather than asking how the earth's surface can be preserved for people, they ask how reservations necessary for the survival of people can be established on an earth that has been reshaped for the sake of industrial outputs.

The Elusive Threshold

Paradoxically, the concept of a traffic-optimal top speed for transport seems capricious or fanatical to the confirmed passenger, whereas it looks like the flight of the bird to the donkey driver. Four or six times the speed of a man on foot constitutes a threshold too low to be deemed worthy of consideration by the habitual passenger and too high to convey the sense of a *limit* to the three-quarters of humanity who still get around on their own power.

All those who plan, finance, or engineer other people's housing, transportation, or education, belong to the passenger class. Their claim to power is derived from the value their employers place on acceleration. Social scientists can build a computer model of traffic in Calcutta or Santiago, and engineers can design monorail webs according to abstract notions of traffic flow. Since these planners are true believers in problem solving by industrial design, the real solution for traffic congestion is beyond their grasp. Their belief in the effectiveness of power blinds them to the disproportionately greater effectiveness of abstaining from its use. Traffic engineers have yet to combine in one simulation model the mobility of people with that of vehicles. The transportation engineer cannot conceive of the possibility of renouncing speed and slowing down for the sake of permitting time-and-destination-optimal traffic flow. He would never entertain the thought of programming his computer on the stipulation that no motorized vehicle within any city should ever overtake the speed of a velocipede. The development expert who looks down compassionately from his Land-Rover on the Indian peasant herding his pigs to market refuses to acknowledge the relative advantage of feet. The expert tends to forget that this man has dispensed ten others in his village from spending time on the road, whereas the engineer and every member of his family separately devote a major part of every day to transportation. For a man who believes that human mobility must be conceived in terms of indefinite progress, there can be no optimal level of traffic but only passing consensus on a given technical level of transportation.

Most Mexicans, not to speak of Indians and Chinese, are in a position inverse to that of the confirmed passenger. The critical threshold is entirely beyond what all but a few of them know or expect. They still belong to the class of the self-powered. Some of them have a lingering memory of a motorized adventure, but most of them have no personal experience of traveling at or above the critical speed. In the two typical Mexican states of Guerrero and Chiapas, less than one per cent of the population moved even once over ten miles in less than one hour during 1970. The vehicles into which people in these areas are sometimes crowded render traffic indeed more convenient, but barely faster than the speed of a bicycle. The third-class bus does not separate the farmer from his pig, and it takes them both to market without inflicting any loss of weight, but this acquaintance with motorized 'comfort' does not amount to dependence on destructive speed.

The order of magnitude in which the critical threshold of speed can be found is too low to be taken seriously by the passenger, and too high to concern the peasant. It is so obvious it cannot be easily seen. The proposal of a limit to speed within this order of magnitude engenders stubborn opposition. It exposes the addiction of industrialized men to ever-higher doses of energy, while it asks those who are still sober to abstain from something they have yet to taste.

To propose counterfoil research is not only a scandal, it is also a threat. Simplicity threatens the expert, who supposedly understands just why the commuter train runs at 8:15 and 8:41 and why it must be better to use fuel with certain additives. That a political process could identify a natural dimension, both inescapable and limited, is an idea that lies outside the passenger's world of verities. He has let respect for specialists he does not even know turn into unthinking submission. If a political resolution could be found for problems created by experts in the field of traffic, then perhaps the same remedy could be applied to problems of education, medicine, or urbanization. If the order of magnitude of traffic-optimal vehicular velocities could be determined by laymen actively participating in an ongoing political process, then the foundation on which the framework of every industrial society is built would be shattered. To propose such research is politically subversive. It calls in question the overarching consensus on the need for more transportation which now allows the proponents of public ownership to define themselves as political adversaries of the proponents of private enterprise.

Degrees of Self-powered Mobility

A century ago, the ball-bearing was invented. It reduced the coefficient of friction by a factor of a thousand. By applying a well-calibrated ball-bearing between two Neolithic millstones, a man could now grind in a day what took his ancestors a week. The ball-bearing also made possible the bicycle, allowing the wheel – probably the last of the great Neolithic inventions – finally to become useful for self-powered mobility.

Man, unaided by any tool, gets around quite efficiently. He carries one gram of his weight over a kilometer in ten minutes by expending 0.75 calories. Man on his feet is thermodynamically more efficient than any motorized vehicle and most animals. For his weight, he performs more work in locomotion than rats or oxen, less than horses or sturgeon. At this rate of efficiency man settled the world and made its history. At this rate peasant societies spend less than 5 per cent and nomads less than 8 per cent of their respective social time budgets outside the home or the encampment.

Man on a bicycle can go three or four times faster than the pedestrian, but uses five times less energy in the process. He carries one gram of his weight over a kilometer of flat road at an expense of only 0.15 calories. The bicycle is the perfect transducer to match man's metabolic energy to the impedance of locomotion. Equipped with this tool, man outstrips the efficiency of not only all machines but all other animals as well.

The invention of the ball-bearing, the tangent-spoked wheel, and the pneumatic tire taken together can be compared to only three other events in the history of transportation. The invention of the wheel at the dawn of civilization took the load off man's back and put it onto the barrow. The invention and simultaneous application, during the European Middle Ages, of stirrup, shoulder harness, and horseshoe increased the thermodynamic efficiency of the horse by a factor of up to five, and changed the economy of medieval Europe: it made frequent plowing possible and thus introduced rotation agriculture; it brought more distant fields into the reach of the peasant, and thus permitted landowners to move from six-family hamlets into one-hundred family villages, where they could live around the church, the square, the jail, and – later – the school; it allowed the cultivation of northern soils and shifted the center of power into cold climates. The building of the first oceangoing vessels by the Portuguese in the fifteenth century, under the aegis of developing European capitalism, laid the solid foundations for a globe-spanning culture and market.

The invention of the ball-bearing signaled a fourth revolution. This revolution was unlike that, supported by the stirrup, which raised the knight onto his horse, and unlike that, supported by the galleon, which enlarged the horizon of the king's captains. The ball-bearing signaled a true crisis, a true political choice. It created an option between more freedom in equity and more speed. The bearing is an equally fundamental ingredient of two new types of locomotion, respectively symbolized by the bicycle and the car. The bicycle lifted man's auto-mobility into a new order, beyond which progress is theoretically not possible. In contrast, the accelerating individual capsule enabled societies to engage in a ritual of progressively paralyzing speed.

The monopoly of a ritual application over a potentially useful device is nothing new. Thousands of years ago, the wheel took the load off the carrier slave, but it did so only on the Eurasian land mass. In Mexico, the wheel was well known, but never applied to transport. It served exclusively for the construction of carriages for toy gods. The taboo on wheelbarrows in America before Cortes is no more puzzling than the taboo on bicycles in modern traffic.

It is by no means necessary that the invention of the ball bearing continue to serve the increase of energy use and thereby produce time scarcity, space consumption, and class privilege. If the new order of self-powered mobility offered by the bicycle were protected against devaluation, paralysis, and risk to the limbs of the rider, it would be possible to guarantee optimal shared mobility to all people and put an end to the imposition of maximum privilege and exploitation. It would be possible to control the patterns of urbanization if the organization of space were constrained by the power man has to move through it.

Bicycles are not only thermodynamically efficient, they are also cheap. With his much lower salary, the Chinese acquires his durable bicycle in a fraction of the working hours an American devotes to the purchase of his obsolescent car. The cost of public utilities needed to facilitate bicycle traffic versus the price of an infrastructure tailored to high speeds is proportionately even less than the price differential of the vehicles used in the two systems. In the bicycle system, engineered roads are necessary only at certain points of dense traffic, and people who live far from the surfaced path are not thereby automatically isolated as they would be if they depended on cars or trains. The bicycle has extended man's radius without shunting him onto roads he cannot walk. Where he cannot ride his bike, he can usually push it.

The bicycle also uses little space. Eighteen bikes can be parked in the place of one car, thirty of them can move along in the space devoured by a single automobile. It takes three lanes of a given size to move 40,000 people across a bridge in one hour by using automated trains, four to move them on buses, twelve to move them in their cars, and only two lanes for them to pedal across on bicycles. Of all these vehicles, only the bicycle really allows people to go from door to door without walking. The cyclist can reach new destinations of his choice without his tool creating new locations from which he is barred.

Bicycles let people move with greater speed without taking up significant amounts of scarce space, energy, or time. They can spend fewer hours on each mile and still travel more miles in a year. They can get the benefit of technological break-throughs without putting undue claims on the schedules, energy, or space of others. They become masters of their own movements without blocking those of their fellows. Their new tool creates only those demands which it can also satisfy. Every increase in motorized speed creates new demands on space and time. The use of the bicycle is self-limiting. It allows people to create a new relationship between their life-space and their life-time, between their territory and the pulse of their being, without destroying their inherited balance. The advantages of modern self-powered traffic are obvious, and ignored. That better traffic runs faster is asserted, but never proved. Before they ask people to pay for it, those who propose acceleration should try to display the evidence for their claim.

A grisly contest between bicycles and motors is just coming to an end. In Vietnam, a hyperindustrialized army tried to conquer, but could not overcome, a people organized around bicycle speed. The lesson should be clear. High-energy armies can annihilate people – both those they defend and those against whom they are launched – but they are of very limited use to a people which defends itself. It remains to be seen if the Vietnamese will apply what they learned in war to an economy of peace, if they will be willing to protect the values that made their victory possible. The dismal likelihood is that the victors, for the sake of industrial progress and increased energy consumption, will tend to defeat themselves by destroying that structure of equity, rationality, and autonomy into which American bombers forced them by depriving them of fuels, motors, and roads.

Dominant versus Subsidiary Motors

People are born almost equally mobile. Their natural ability speaks for the personal liberty of each one to go wherever he or she wants to go. Citizens of a society founded on the notion of equity will demand the protection of this right against any abridgment. It should be irrelevant to them by what means the exercise of personal mobility is denied, whether by imprisonment, bondage to an estate, revocation of a passport, or enclosure within an environment that encroaches on a person's native ability to move in order to make him a consumer of transport. This inalienable right of free movement does not lapse just because most of our contemporaries have strapped themselves into ideological seat belts. Man's natural capacity for transit emerges as the only yardstick by which to measure the contribution transport can make to traffic: there is only so much transport that traffic can bear. It remains to be outlined how we can distinguish those forms of transport that cripple the power to move from those that enhance it.

Transportation can abridge traffic in three ways: by breaking its flow, by creating isolated sets of destinations, and by increasing the loss of time due to traffic. I have already argued that the key to the relation between transport and traffic is the speed of vehicles. I have described how, past a certain threshold of speed, transport has gone on to obstruct traffic in these three ways. It blocks mobility by cluttering up the environment with vehicles and roads. It transforms geography into a pyramid of circuits sealed off from one another according to levels of acceleration. It expropriates life-time at the behest of speed.

If beyond a certain threshold transport obstructs traffic, the inverse is also true: below some level of speed, motorized vehicles can complement or improve traffic by permitting people to do things they could not do on foot or on bicycle. A well-developed transportation system running at top speeds of 25 mph would have allowed Fix to chase Phileas Fogg around the world in less than half of eighty days. Motors can be used to transport the sick, the lame, the old, and the just plain lazy. Motor pulleys can lift people over hills, but they can do so peacefully only if they do not push the climber off the path. Trains can extend the range of travel, but can do so with justice only if people have not only equal transportation but equal free time to come closer to each other. The time engaged in travel must be, as much as possible, the traveler's own: only insofar as motorized transport remains limited to speeds which leave it subsidiary to autonomous transit can a traffic-optimal transportation system be developed.

A limit on the power and therefore on the speed of motors does not by itself insure those who are weaker against exploitation by the rich and powerful, who can still devise means to live and work at better located addresses, travel with retinue in plush carriages, and reserve a special lane for doctors and members of the central committee. But at a sufficiently limited maximum speed, this is an unfairness which can be reduced or even corrected by political means: by grassroots control over taxes, routes, vehicles, and their schedules in the community. At unlimited top speed neither public ownership of the means of transportation nor technical improvements in their control can ever eliminate growing and unequal exploitation. A transportation industry is the key to optimal production of traffic, but only if it does not exercise its radical monopoly over that personal mobility which is intrinsically and primarily a value in use.

Underequipment, Overdevelopment and Mature Technology

The combination of transportation and transit that constitutes traffic has provided us with an example of socially optimal per capita wattage and of the need for politically chosen limits on it. But traffic can also be viewed as but one model for the convergence of worldwide development goals, and as a criterion by which to distinguish those countries that are lamely underequipped from those that are destructively overindustrialized.

A country can be classified as underequipped if it cannot outfit each citizen with a bicycle or provide a five-speed transmission as a bonus for anyone who wants to pedal others around. It is underequipped if it cannot provide good roads for the cycle, or free motorized public transportation (though at bicycle speed!) for those who want to travel for more than a few hours in succession. No technical, economic, or ecological reason exists why such backwardness should be tolerated anywhere in 1975. It would be a scandal if the natural mobility of a people were forced to stagnate on a pre-bicycle level against its will.

A country can be classified as overindustrialized when its social life is dominated by the transportation industry, which has come to determine its class privileges, to accentuate its time scarcity, and to tie its people more tightly to the tracks it has laid out for them.

Beyond underequipment and overindustrialization, there is a place for the world of postindustrial effectiveness, where the industrial mode of production complements other autonomous forms of production. There is a place, in other words, for a world of technological maturity. In terms of traffic, it is the world of those who have tripled the extent of their daily horizon by lifting themselves onto their bicycles. It is just as much the world marked by a variety of subsidiary motors available for the occasions when a bicycle is not enough and when an extra push will limit neither equity nor freedom. And it is, too, the world of the long voyage: a world where every place is open to every person, at his own pleasure and speed, without haste or fear, by means of vehicles that cross distances without breaking with the earth which man walked for hundreds of thousands of years on his own two feet.

Underequipment keeps people frustrated by inefficient labor and invites the enslavement of man by man. Overindustrialization enslaves people to the tools they worship, fattens professional hierarchs on bits and on watts, and invites the translation of unequal power into huge income differentials. It imposes the same net transfers of power on the productive relations of every society, no matter what creed the managers profess, no matter what rain-dance, what penitential ritual they conduct. Technological maturity permits a society to steer a course equally free of either enslavement. But beware – that course is not charted. Technological maturity permits a variety of political choices and cultures. The variety diminishes, of course, as a community allows industry to grow at the cost of autonomous production. Reasoning alone can offer no precise measure for the level of postindustrial effectiveness and technological maturity appropriate to a concrete society. It can only indicate in dimensional terms the range into which these technological characteristics must fit. It must be left to a historical community engaged in its own political process to decide when programming, space distortion, time scarcity, and inequality cease to be worth its while. Reasoning can identify speed as the critical factor in traffic. Reasoning combined with experimentation can identify the order of magnitude at which vehicular speed turns into a sociopolitical determinant. No genius, no expert, no club of elites can set limits to industrial outputs that will be politically feasible. The need for such limits as an alternative to disaster is the strongest argument in favor of radical technology.

Only when the speed limits of vehicles reflect the enlightened self-interest of a political community can these limits become operative. Obviously this interest cannot even be expressed in a society where one class monopolizes not only transportation but communication, medicine, education, and weapons as well. It does not matter if this power is held by legal owners or by entrenched managers of an industry that is legally owned by the workers. This power must be re-appropriated and submitted to the sound judgment of the common man. The reconquest of power starts with the recognition that expert knowledge blinds the secretive bureaucrat to the obvious way of dissolving the energy crisis, just as it blinded him to the obvious solution to the war in Vietnam.

There are two roads from where we are to technological maturity: one is the road of liberation from affluence; the other is the road of liberation from dependence. Both roads have the same destination: the social restructuring of space that offers to each person the constantly renewed experience that the center of the world is where he stands, walks, and lives.

Liberation from affluence begins on the traffic islands where the rich run into one another. The well-sped are tossed from one island to the next and are offered but the company of fellow passengers en route to somewhere else. This solitude of plenty would begin to break down as the traffic islands gradually expanded and people began to recover their native power to move around the place where they lived. Thus, the impoverished environment of the traffic island could embody the beginnings of social reconstruction, and the people who now call themselves rich would break with bondage to overefficient transport on the day they came to treasure the horizon of their traffic islands, now fully grown, and to dread frequent shipments from their homes.

Liberation from dependence starts at the other end. It breaks the constraints of village and valley and leads beyond the boredom of narrow horizons and the stifling oppression of a world closed in on itself. To expand life beyond the radius of tradition without scattering it to the winds of acceleration is a goal that any poor country could achieve within a few years, but it is a goal that will be reached only by those who reject the offer of unchecked industrial development made in the name of an ideology of indefinite energy consumption.

Liberation from the radical monopoly of the transportation industry is possible only through the institution of a political process that demystifies and disestablishes speed and limits traffic-related public expenditures of money, time, and space to the pursuit of equal mutual access. Such a process amounts to public guardianship over a means of production to keep this means from turning into a fetish for the majority and an end for the few. The political process, in turn, will never engage the support of a vast majority unless its goals are set with reference to a standard that can be publicly and operationally verified. The recognition of a socially critical threshold of the energy quantum incorporated in a commodity, such as a passenger mile, provides such a standard. A society that tolerates the transgression of this threshold inevitably diverts its resources from the production of means that can be shared equitably and transforms them into fuel for a sacrificial flame that victimizes the majority. On the other hand, a society that limits the top speed of its vehicles in accordance with this threshold fulfills a necessary – though by no means a sufficient – condition for the political pursuit of equity.

Liberation which comes cheap to the poor will cost the rich dear, but they will pay its price once the acceleration of their transportation systems grinds traffic to a halt. A concrete analysis of traffic betrays the truth underlying the energy crisis: the impact of industrially packaged quanta of energy on the social environment tends to be degrading, exhausting, and enslaving, and these effects come into play even before those which threaten the pollution of the physical environment and the extinction of the race. The crucial point at which these effects can be reversed is not, however, a matter of deduction, but of decision.

THE SOCIAL
CONSTRUCTION
OF ENERGY

Opening talk to a Seminar on
"The Basic Option within any Future Low-Energy Society"
held at *El Colegio de México*, México, July 1983.

by Ivan Illich

THERE IS LITTLE in common between "e" when a physicist writes it and "energy" when the word is used by an economist, politician or windmill fan. "E" is an algorithm, "energy" is a loaded word. "E" is meaningful only within a formula, "energy" is charged with hidden implications: it refers to a subtle something which has the ability to make nature do work. Even the engineer who routinely handles megawatts talks of "energy" when he speaks to his client. Energy now, as work formerly, has become something which individuals and societies need. It is a symbol that fits our age, the symbol of that which is both abundant and scarce.

The theoretical notion and the social construct were born as Siamese twins. By the end of the nineteenth century, aged barely fifty, they had become antagonistic look-alikes. "E" had matured in the hothouse of labs. Each new trick "e" learned to play, each new twist it was taught, has been carefully monitored. In the course of its history, "e" has embedded into its own theory the rules by which the symbol may be used. In Einstein's words it became part "of the theory which decides what the physicist sees." "Energy" in the meantime rose to the throne of the Almighty, and became the metaphor for what is now called "basic needs". "E" became abstract, beyond imagination. "Energy" became both mysterious and trivial, beyond examination and seemingly unworthy of it. Today the twinborn determine two types of discourse, so strange that they just barely translate into each other.

I do not want to add to the knowledge about "e". I am also not dealing here with free and bound energy, that is, sexuality in Sigmund Freud; this theme I take up in a separate essay. Nor do I want to comment here on the attempts to interpret the "working" of the social order in terms of thermodynamics, as Georgescu-Roegen has done. Further, I do not deal with those historians who have tried to complement economic history with historical energetics; with Ostwald at the turn of the century, Leslie White towards its middle and many energy-mystics today, for whom progress reflects society's ability to appropriate energy. The interpretation of economics as a special case of thermodynamics, the interpretation of society as a system of self-regulating energy exchanges, or the attempt to interpret social evolution as increased social control over energy flows – all these I consider seductive but limping analogies. My reason for dealing with the history of "energy" is different from all these; I discover in the emergence of this verbal symbol the means by which nature has been interpreted as a domain governed by the assumption of scarcity, and thus human beings could be re-defined as nature's ever needy clients. Once the universe itself is placed under the regime of scarcity, *homo* is no longer born under the stars but under the axioms of economics. To get at the matter I must review briefly the core meanings of "energy", how it was transmogrified from human vigor to nature's capital. In Greek, the word "energy" is both frequent and strong. It might best be rendered in English as "being on the make", with all the shades this expression carries. In its Latin version, *in actu*, the term is of central importance in medieval philosophy, meaning form, perfection, act, in contrast to mere possibility. In ordinary English, the word first appears in the sixteenth century. For Elizabethans, energy means the vigor of an utterance, the force of an expression, always the quality of a personal presence. A hundred years later the word can qualify an impersonal impact: the power of an argument or the ability of church music to generate an effect in the soul. The term is still used exclusively for psychic effects, although only for those engendered by either a person or a thing.

During the seventeenth century, the attempt got underway to quantify nature's forces. Leibnitz spoke of a magnitude that remains intact whatever happens, "like money when it is changed." In the eighteenth century, the *vis viva*, life-force of the universe became a quantity of motion, an important concept of natural philosophers: collisions, springs, rolling balls were observed, and each language in Europe was enriched by several words to designate the different kinds of power or efficacy passed on, and variously expressed as "m.v", "m.v²", "(1/2)m.v²", This *vis* was renamed by Thomas Young and called "energy."

In 1807, he wrote that "energy may be applied with great property to the mass or the weight of a body into the square number expressing its velocity." Paradoxically, the term energy, used for the preceding 300 years to designate the forcefulness of a face or the liveliness of a statement was first used to designate the "force of nature" precisely at the time when – in all the natural sciences – nature's vitality, its "Lebenskraft", was being systematically denied. Young's usage, however, did not gain acceptance. It took another forty years before energy entered the terminology of physics, and then – in opposition to Young – to designate a "something" in contrast to a "force". Energy is distinguished in modern physics from force as the integral from its function.

Only through this distinction did energy come into its own. It had never been attributed to nature, as long as nature was spoken of as "mother". By 1844, nature, in Liebig's words, had become the one "matrix" of distinct forces such as electricity, heat, light, and magnetism that could be measured in units of work. This shift of language is uncannily close to a shift of language in obstetrics. Until the early eighteenth century, it was women who bore children; and women who were delivered of them by women. After 1820, it is a bio-engineer, the gynaecologist, who delivers the child from the matrix, and the child grows up into the work-force.

During the first half of the nineteenth century, physics construed something akin to the division of labour: value equivalents between heat, electricity and mechanical movements were measured. One Englishman boiled water by drilling a canon and related the amount of steam pressure produced in the effort made by the horse turning the drill. Another one got heat by rubbing two blocks of ice against each other, and reported the amount of water obtained in the effort expended. The search for something like a gold standard in nature thus led to a new kind of experimental metaphysics: to laboratory proofs of entities that cannot be observed. The objective existence of something which just changes its form in ever more precisely observed and measured appearances became itself the new scientific mythology. Though no one, of course, observed it – and for a decade there was no agreement on the term which should name it – Julius Robert von Mayer (1842), Hermann von Helmholtz (1847), William Thomson (Lord Kelvin) and several others, working independently from each other, defined this something as nature's ability to perform work. "Work" in these five years from 1842 to 1847 became a physical magnitude, and energy its sources. Work was defined as the production of a physical change, and energy was assumed as its metaphysical cause.

It might be important to recall that during the second quarter of the nineteenth century the same scientific myth found its expression in three images: the womb became the source of life, the universe the source of energy, and the population a source of labour force. I here focus on the parallel traits of the second and third. As "Arbeitskraft" was imputed to human activity insofar as it is productive in the economy, energy was imputed to nature insofar as it produces work. Through the imputation of energy, nature was recast in the image of the newly constituted human as worker. Nature now understood as the depository and matrix of a work force called energy mirrored the proletariat, the matrix of available labour force. And the steam engine lurked behind all reality.

The artifact that could serve as unifying symbol had been the clock, under the absolute rulers of the sixteenth and seventeenth centuries. With its automata dancing at the hour and a cosmic theater of spheres, the ruler's clock was not primarily a means to measure time. It was the spectacle of rational harmony in medicine, pageantry and state; it demonstrated central authority in the cosmos over bodies, planets and subjects. But a clock's wheels that had neither liberty nor autonomy became abhorrent to the political and religious protestants, especially in late seventeenth century England. The self-regulating machine became the symbol of constitutional monarchy, the image of a new order based on countervailing forces and the dynamic balance of supply and demand. However, these Cartesian machines were not meant to work. The new machine which drives the thermodynamic age is meant to work: it symbolizes the age of production, of input and output. Henceforth nature, the womb, population, and even the clock of old, are perceived as devices that work. The steam engine first, then the dynamo which, invented by Faraday in 1831, was by accident inverted at the Vienna Exposition of 1873 and became the electric motor. Finally, the moving internal combustion plant completed the third successive stage of the modern world which "works".

In 1827, Joule was looking for a word to designate "the unit of work done by a unit of fuel". He picked the word "duty" as the measure of a machine's efficiency. The reduction of duty to the performance of productive work for men and reproduction for women, so characteristic for the second quarter of the nineteenth century, thus also embraced the machine. By the end of this short span, "the whole of so-called world history is nothing more than the production of man through human work," to quote Marx (*die Erzeugung des Menschen durch die menschliche Arbeit*). The simultaneous invention of these two distinct "potentials for work", energy and labour-power, deserves to be explored. This, however, makes it necessary to return to the history of "e" to avoid any confusion of it with "energy".

In 1872, the first attempt was undertaken by Mach to write the history of the "principle of conservation" formulated fully twenty-five years earlier by Helmholtz. Mach did not write on the conservation of "energy", but on the conservation of "Arbeit – which is work". The first to undertake explicitly a history of "e" was Max Planck, at the age of twenty-six. He tried to exclude all hypotheses about the constitution of nature or of heat, any reference to the movement of corpuscles or imponderable fluids. He was concerned with the measurement of nature's manifestations in work, and the history of the corresponding accounting system. With his paper, Planck tried and failed to win the first prize at a competition at the Philosophical Faculty of Gottingen in 1884. It was obvious for Planck that the concept of "energy", which he wanted to study in its historical evolution, derived all its meaning in physics from the principle of "conservation of energy" as the idea, that "it is impossible to get work done without compensation" (*die Leistung von Arbeit kann nicht ... ohne irgend eine Kompensation erfolgen*). Planck shows that the idea had been conceived and formulated in the mid-1840s, and that by the sixties there was no more doubt about its validity. I have not found in this early paper of Max Planck even the slightest suspicion that the language used about the principles of physics was decidedly socio-genetic.

However, at the same time, Mach had already begun to pry apart "energy" from "e," and had thus taken the necessary steps for the divorce which meant the end of fifty years of *classical* thermodynamics. For Mach, it is inadmissible to postulate something like a work force behind observed phenomena, unless the scientist is able to verify its existence by direct experiment. Mach did not deny the convenience of such a hypothesis; he only requested that the person using it be aware that what he uses is a supposition. The choice of one among several applicable hypotheses, according to Mach, should be made entirely on the grounds of the elegance with which such a concept – as, for instance, "energy" – fits into the formulas that connect observed events. His controversy with H.R. Hertz made this clear: Hertz had described the transverse wave nature of electromagnetic action through space, in which "e" was left out. Mach objected to this, not because he found fault with Hertz's demonstration, but because using "e" would have allowed a more elegant statement. Einstein, throughout his life, was unambiguous about entities like "e": they "cannot be derived from experience by logic but must be understood as free creations of the human spirit." By the beginning of the century, "e" was recognized by those who used it as such a construct to designate the state of a field. Kantians interpreted it as the physical formulation of the principle of causality. Poincaré reduced it to a mere tautology. By 1920, the few who still reached for a meta-mathematical interpretation of the "e" explained it as the consequence of a symmetry within fields or as a characteristic of the homogeneity of time, something which in relativity and quantum mechanics plays a role faintly reminiscent of the golden rule in Greek architecture, the *logos*.

To keep as sober as Mach or Einstein was not easy as theoretical modern physics acquired prestige. People left outside the charmed circle around "e" looked towards the academic Alchemists as the source of ultimate riches or as initiates into ultimate mystique. Not a few physicists began to pander to the public. Energy was presented as the sold attribute of ultimate reality. Under the name of "energetism", F. Paulsen (1892) had already developed the idea that ethics, much more than mathematics, had to be understood as the other side of physics: both dealt with the perfection of being through its activity, its work. The outstanding representative of the new "energetics" was, of course, Wilhelm Ostwald. Nobel Prize laureate in 1908, editor of one of the most prestigious scientific journals, publisher of 230 volumes of scientific classics, creator of the logarithmic classification of colours; this man dedicated his main work to E. Mach. In several major books, he presented "energy" as the only real substance, the common substrate of body and soul. He applied the second principle of thermodynamics to economics and ethics. "All life is a competition for free energy whose accessible quantity is always in scarce supply" (1913). Valuation, choice and action (*das Wollen* – more precisely, "willing") can be reduced to energetic terms encompassing material and spiritual reality. From 1883, Ostwald published his Sunday sermons; later he became the president of the World Monist Association. What in Ostwald sounds like the lucubrations of a physicist turned quasi-philosopher had lost its news value by World War II. Without the need to make much ado about it, Heisenberg formulates the same convictions in his Gifford Lectures of 1956/7 in the form of a creed: "The substance out of which all elementary particles and all things are made ... that which causes change, and changes, but is never lost ... that which can be transformed into movement, heat, light, tension ... that is energy." As "e" became esoteric, an increasing number of physicists came to act as gurus who popularized its real nature. Once famous physicists had lent their prestige to the interpretation of energy as nature's ultimate Kapital, the principle of "the conservation of energy" became the cosmological confirmation of the postulate of scarcity. The principle of contradiction was "operationalized"; it was restated in the formula that "you can't get a free lunch." By a cosmic extension of the assumption of scarcity, the world visible and invisible was turned into a zero sum game, as if Jehovah, with a big bang, had created *das Kapital.*

Both nineteenth century energetism, that tried to reduce value to energy, and twentieth century energetic monism, still with us in the exoteric Heisenberg, adhere to the myth that science was a rational undertaking. This changed with F. Capra's *Tao of Physics* (1975). The discovery of energy now reflects an evolution of human consciousness (E. Jantsch, *The Evolutionary Vision*, 1981), and the recovery of mystical experience as a superior form of knowledge (M. Talbot, *Mysticism and the New Physics*, 1981). In this view, the cosmology of modern physics converges with old oriental intuitions in China (G. Zukov, *The Dancing Wu-Li Masters* 1979) and Advaita Vedanta (R.H. Jones, *Mysticism and Science* 1980). The Alchemists are perhaps turning into theologians. And the theology of "energy" is as alien to my precise concern as the mathematics of "e".

I am interested not in the theology but in the superstitions about energy. This first seminar on the social construction of energy is being held at the *Colegio de Mexico*, and this has for me a special significance. The library of this institution holds an immense deposit of Latin American superstitions. In thirty years of labor, I have helped to assemble this stuff. Superstitious religiosity has been for three decades my hobby – neither theology, nor just any popular religiosity, but superstition. I learned from Kriss-Rettenbeck to call superstition the popular beliefs and forms of behaviour which come into existence under the aegis, the shield, of a church. Therefore, they can be studied in contrast to the dogmas taught and the rituals propagated by the organization, the ideologies promoted by the Church. In this narrow sense, superstition exists only in the shadow of a powerful church. In this sense, superstition is not just any syncretism, but the use popular religiosity makes out of the Church. This scabrous background led me to the history of "energy" as a superstition in modern civic religiosity. The fathers around 1847 revealed it, the Ostwalds preached it and the laity accepted the message of a spiritual awakening to a cosmos defined by the assumptions of scarcity.

There can be no history of energy as a popular construct without a history of work, and vice versa. The destinies of the two words have been intertwined ever since they dawned in the sphere of keywords. But the two are stars of very different types. Energy has been sighted by Young like a comet which is far off, and then changed its position as it grew brighter. Work is a well-known fixed star which lighted up as a nova so powerful that it led to the renaming of entire constellations. From Joules to Planck, energy was academic. After Ostwald, it became the "holy", the "arcanum" of a secularizing world, a "power" which physicists could tame. Slowly, the Einsteins replaced the Eiffels as public heroes, as the lab replaced the drawing board in prestige. All this time energy remained positively charged. The blame for the bomb was fixed on the atom. When oil became political, energy became the equivalent for fuel: watts for machines and calories for people. In May 1972, the editor of *Le Monde* asked me to drop the opening sentence of an editorial that he wanted to publish. I had written, "the words 'energy crisis' conceal a contradiction and consecrate an illusion." The editor claims that the two words were unheard of in France. Shortly afterwards, he printed a ten-page special supplement that carried just that title.

The dates when energy was charged with new meanings are easy to remember. This is not so for the key word, work. Work meant deed, task, effort, duty. It always referred to concrete action, or to the result of this action in "a good piece of work." Towards the middle of the eighteenth century, work for the first time could mean the aggregate of such actions. Physiocrats compounded the useful activities of the king's subjects and related them to the well being of the realm. The relationship between well-being and the conglomerate of activities was not yet perceived as a result of the "productivity" of work. Work was seen as the factor that accelerates the circulation of goods, and this agitation was perceived as the condition for the accumulation of riches. Though not productive, work was, by 1750, recognized as a decisive factor in the creation of wealth.

The idea that work did not just permit the accumulation of wealth, but could create economic value we owe to Adam Smith. For Smith, the labour force – work in the abstract – became the true measure of the exchange value of all goods. Now, labour had become something which could be measured as an aggregate: "the annual labour of every nation is the fund which originally supplies it with all necessaries and conveniences of life" (*Wealth of Nations*, 1776). "Profit and rent constitute a deduction from values created by labour alone" was an idea of Smith on which Ricardo elaborated to distinguish the forms of labour: live work, freely available from people, and past labour bound up as capital which could be put to work. By 1821 Ricardo recognized that capital, in the form of machinery, could replace live labour and thus become injurious to the working class. He elaborated a cost theory of value: with the reversible equivalence between the two forms of labour he remained within the field of the observable. It never occurred to him to connect profit to the expropriation of value which is drawn from a meta-economical sphere.

Political economy inquires into the matrix from which value flows. The step from Ricardo to Marx can be compared to the step from Sadi Carnot to Helmholtz. Carnot in 1824 examined the moving power of fire. He established a set of equations that show how steam engines work. His equations still hold. The validity of his demonstration depends exclusively on what he had observed: temperature differentials and work performance. With Helmholtz, we get an explanation of *why* steam drives the piston. Work is the result of the transfer of energy from coal to wheel, and that is the way late twentieth century textbooks still define it. In economics, Ricardo, a contemporary of Sadi Carnot's, valued work at the price paid for the worker's time. Twenty years later, as Helmholtz worked on his epoch-making paper, young Marx traced the source of economic value. He developed the theory that explains how the employer can appropriate the surplus value of labour. For Marx, the economy runs on the positive difference between the total labor time used in production and that part of it that covers the cost of the reproduction of the work force. For Smith and Ricardo, what the worker sold was his service, his concrete work. In Marx, he sells his labour-power, his *Arbeit-Kraft*, part of which is expropriated by the capitalist. The parallel between the potential to work possessed by nature and by the proletariat can be further developed. When the engineer taps energy, this energy produces two things: work and random heat, chaos, which latter Clausius called entropy. Something analogous happens when the capitalist taps labour power, which produces two things: surplus value for him and the income to the worker that goes up in untidy reproduction. Thus, the population saw itself reduced to the matrix of a labour force, and nature was reduced to be the matrix of energy. Gynaecologists redefined women as those human beings whose very nature has destined them to the reproduction of "new life".

However, political economy soon became as irrelevant to economics as energetics to physics. The two might use the same terms, but with different meanings. The "labour force" that appears in a socialist manpower report means the same that it means in a report from the World Bank. But just as monist professors of physics preached vulgar energetics, Marxist economists love to pontificate on the labour theory of value.

Quite independently from their meanings in science and structured ideologies, the two words work and energy became key-words of contemporary language. Both became strong persuasive words which give a moral and social interpretation to the sentence in which they occur. That work acts as such a key word has been recognized. The "right to work", the "dignity of work", a "workers republic", "labour" and, especially, "unemployment" carry direct and strong ethical connotations. We are aware of their recent origin and their distinctiveness is unique for the different epochs we can remember. This has not been so for energy. It has been overlooked that the word energy functions as a collage of meanings whose persuasiveness is based on the myth that what it expresses is natural. Thus, surreptitiously, our lifestyle could become energy intensive. The right to work and the need for gas could be connected. Jobs and watts could be recognized as basic rights because they were both interpreted as basic needs. The modern state could be interpreted as an employment agency with a gun to protect the fuel pump. Politicians could win by the mere promise of more watts and jobs. Development assistance could carry the ideal of "man as an energy guzzling commodity producer" to the ends of the earth, because progress came to mean the replacement of feet by motorized wheels, the replacement of the kitchen garden by frozen foods, the replacement of adobe by cement, the replacement of the trench by the WC. The radical monopoly of our energy-intensive lifestyle over the landscape, culture and language has made the ideal of energy dependence into an inescapable reality. In many places you cannot move any longer without wheels, you cannot eat without a refrigerator, you choke unless you turn on the air conditioner. Thus the need for energy – and not only for jobs – became morally obvious: part of that civic religiosity which lies far beneath the political oppositions in a modern society.

Now, quite suddenly, society is running out of work. Simultaneously, the terms most frequently associated with energy are crisis and scarcity or, more ominously, atom or neutron. Whatever remedies to unemployment are being proposed, they do not inspire much confidence: work-time reduction, job sharing, energy saving, defense spending, ecology – they look like palliatives comparable to chemo-therapy in cancer; if they do add to the survival of our lifestyle, they will also render it more distressing. No doubt, many contemporaries are turning towards the computer as the new panacea. If the computer has an effect on the environment analogous to that of the car, soon you will not be able to do without it: no mail, no tax return, no voting, no purchase without it. An entirely new kind of poverty is on the horizon: the under-informed. While in the sixties poverty could be measured by a low level of wattage, it will soon be measured by low access to or use of the computer. While miserly microprocessors will guard energy-trickles more effectively than cave women nurtured the fire, half of the population will teach the other half how to use the computer. The computer is credited with the capacity to create unsuspected amounts of busywork. We are straight on our way towards an energy-obsessed low energy society in a world that worships work but has nothing for people to do. We cannot break out as long as our principles remain the laws of thermodynamics.

I have dealt elsewhere with the reasons that make it so difficult to recognize work as defined in the nineteenth century as a construct. I have shown that such a thing as genderless work, in theory equally fit for men and women, had not been thought of before. It is impossible to deal with this matter here. My concern here is to mention those conditions which make it difficult to recognize energy for what it is: the ultimate symbol of monist sexism affirming itself within the matrix of the law which says that the male principle cannot be destroyed. I will mention four such obstacles: historical energetics, soft ecology, belief in the objectivity of science and, finally, epistemological sexism.

The first obstacle in recognizing energy as a recent invention is the spectacles with which we are trained to look at the past. Utility companies grind them for us by buying space in the journals, not excluding the highbrows. Typically, the ad shows a middle-aged company scientist who cares for the future of our children. His message is always the same: ... energy is something arcane ... we all need it ... we just cannot but use it ... no one ever has done without it ... unless the man in the ad does research it will soon run out ... and then comes the punch: remember Neanderthal! how he toiled to light fire from a spark; and then look at yourself, you just turn on the light; he carried his water, you switch on the pump ... people always needed energy from Stonehenge to Telsat. It seems that these ads are not without effect, because they do hit a weak spot. The wider the gap that separates the wattage of their reader from that of an Indian, the more obviously silly his needs, the more he is prone to mirror himself in the behaviour of his ancestors. He gloats over pop-science that tells him that Cro-Magnon was as aggressive and sexist as he; he hails Mary Douglas for telling him that he has inherited from old rituals his fear of pollution; he is comforted to learn that Australopithecus was just as dependent on energy as today's Mr. Smith.

The second obstacle to the recognition of energy as an interpretative concept of human existence has been created, at least in part, by the propaganda for the soft path. I feel embarrassed because I did not myself recognize this danger at an earlier time. Fifteen years ago, I worked on a multi-dimensional model of thresholds, beyond which tools become counterproductive. To make my argument, I was then delighted to find others working on energy accounting. I was happy to compare the efficiency of a man with that of a motor, both pushing the same bike – to the clear advantage of the man. I was delighted to belong to the race that had invented the ball bearing and the tire when I found out that, on a bike, I was more "energy efficient" than a sturgeon of my weight. I have since often used the comparison between the energy inputs needed to put a bowl of rice into the hand of a Burmese farmer and onto the table of a NY restaurant. As a tour de force, in terms of "e", these comparisons are certainly useful. But I did not then grasp the power of their reductionist seduction. Because even then I knew how to distinguish between transit and transport, between an automobile person on his or her feet, and the immobile passenger depending on shipment. But I was not then fully aware that by measuring both forms of locomotion in terms of watts I blinded myself and my readers to the essential difference between the two. People and motors do not move through the same kind of space. Auto-mobile people culturally constitute the commons on which they walk, and stay within the range of their feet at the self-limiting rhythm of their bodies. Vehicles tend to annihilate commons into unlimited thoroughfares. By transforming commons into resources for the production of passenger miles, vehicles take the use value out of feet. They homogenize the landscape, make it non-transitable and then catapult people from point to point. By imputing energy-amounts to the man on his feet, I inevitably play into the hands of the ecologist who blurs this distinction, who makes of commons and spatial resources one amalgam. By using energy-amounts to measure the distance covered by medieval peasants and pilgrims I inevitably conjured up the illusion that their milieu, like our environment, was under the regime of scarcity, that they engaged in energy efficient self-transportation.

Once you accept this amalgam you foster the appearance of the ecocrat. He replaces the technocrat whose authority was at least limited to the management of people and social machines. The ecocrat's aims transcend these institutions; his management tools fit nature into their domain. Symbolically, the ecocrat tears down the hedge that separates society from the wild, that boundary that was the traditional seat of the witch. He sees himself as a holist because he encompasses society and its environment as two sub-systems of a whole which works.

The emblem of the new synthesis is the computer. At first sight, it seems a symbol as radically new as the steam engine when it replaced the clock, but this is not so. To enthrone the working machine as the symbol for nature and society, science had to be based on a new presupposition of thermodynamic laws. Neither in theory nor in ideology have the computer and its information theory weakened our moral and social dependence on these. Most so-called alternative currents of thought and of rhetoric bolster the old symbols of scarce value: work, energy, production. The computer is pictured as the great economizer and economist who will sugarcoat work by rendering energy and employment more effective, more decentralized, more flexible and complex. As during the time of the factory, when Right and Left reinforced by their very opposition the assumptions of the age, so now the added opposition of soft and hard path cements society's dependence on the zero-sum game. However, I believe that now more than ever we do have a choice. The computer could become the symbol through which society is split in a new way. I am not speaking here of the "dual economy" which seems anyway to be on the horizon: one low and one high productivity sphere. Independent from this polarization, I speak of a much more profound split. I speak of the recognition within society of two distinct domains: on the one hand, the economy, run under assumptions of our need for commodities, which – no matter how abundant (as for instance, bits) – are by their very nature scarce and, on the other, a slowly disembedding sphere of life to which you gain access simply by unplugging from the thermodynamic assumptions of economics. Let science and artificial intelligence manage production and distribution of those few basic commodities which all need – and of which there can be enough for all. And let most people live as much of their life as they chose, unplugged from work, watts and bits. I am definitely not speaking as a romantic of a return to the woods, or as a Luddite angry at chips. What I envisage is a step beyond Karl Polanyi. Polanyi made me understand the disembedding of a formal economy as the process which could not but destroy the commons until social life and economy came largely to coincide. I am suggesting that we now envisage the disembedding of a new sphere of freedom in which we have exorcised the miserly critters of quite recent creation from the perception of who we are.

However, the discussion to trivialize the economic sphere and subordinate it to a sphere of social freedom runs counter to the major ideologies that have come with belief in energy and work. And, the trivialization of economic values also runs counter to the basic myths on which contemporary science and ethics are built.

This brings us to the third major obstacle to the recognition of energy as an addicting illusion: our unwillingness to recognize the very foundations of science as the contemporary legitimate myths. J.C. Maxwell of "cosmic ether" fame had already recognized the principle of conservation of energy for what it was: a *law* in the sense that it is a "science producing doctrine". Like Planck, his contemporary, he knew that this so-called law of nature was first recognized, and only then was energy chosen as the expression of its value. Historically and psychological, the *rule* that nature, like citizens of the nineteenth century, must live in the matrix of a zero-sum game was prior to the *value* at stake in this game. Only then did that value take the form of a function, namely "e", or a "goody". Progress in the social sciences went in the same direction. Social interactions were reduced to exchanges, and subjects to role players between whom these exchanges take place. The perfectly neutral medium of exchange is implied in all science based on conservation, and energy is its paradigm.

Finally, there is a fourth reason that makes it almost impossible to unplug from the assumptions of energy and of work without seeming to be immoral. Our society's image of the human being depends on them. And this ideal of the human being – which I consider sexist – most women today share with men. They find it as difficult as men to recognize the ideal as sexist. This human being has the potential to work. Conceptually, it acquired this ability sometime between the generation of Carnot and Ricardo, and the generation of Marx and Helmholtz. Up to that time, men did not do what women did, and vice versa. Up to that time in each community, tasks and tools were split in two halves and, in each community, the split was a different one. This split was transcended through the constitution of the labour force – in theory and in practice. The *genderless worker* was called for by the matrix of the work-force, as energy by the law of conservation. And this worker – he or she – inhabits a universe in which everything is made of one stuff only: energy.

In a masterly study, Brian Easlea (*Witch-hunting, Magic & the New Philosophy*, 1980) traced the erection of this universe from the witch-hunts to the constitution of the Victorian woman. He describes how, during the seventeenth century, natural philosophers began to banish life conceptually from the cosmos, and how they minimized the role of women in conception. Step by step, they succeeded to declare matter pure, inert nature – agitated by the *vis viva*. They succeeded to reduce matter to pure *mater*, the amorphous mother of things, a pure womb in formless readiness for the conception of paternal powers; a mere framework within which virile force could give rise to all things. Materia/mater in this process became logically unknowable, because amorphous and physically unobservable, nothing but a shapeless presupposition. The study of this necessary and complementary principle of all existence was thus by definition excluded from science. Science became the knowledge of virile forces and the shapes they take. In the 1840s, their complement reappeared as the matrix and the law that exalts the conservation of virile energy as the first law of the cosmos and the foundation of modern science.

Ivan Illich (1926–2002) was an Austrian philosopher, Roman Catholic priest, and critic of technological society and the unacknowledged axioms of the modern mind. He was appointed vice-rector of the Catholic University in Puerto Rico in 1956. In 1961, Illich founded the Centro Intercultural de Documentación (CIDOC) at Cuernavaca, Mexico, where he developed many of his ideas. He is the author of many books including *Celebration of Awareness, Tools for Conviviality, The Right to Useful Unemployment, Energy and Equity, Shadow Work, Gender, H₂O and the Waters of Forgetfulness, ABC: The Alphabetization of the Popular Mind, Disabling Professions, Deschooling Society* and *In the Mirror of the Past.*

How fresh they are! These essays of Ivan Illich date back to the 1970s, an epoch of early disenchantment with industrialism and economic growth. Forty years later, it is striking how entrenched in our minds the myths of modernity still are. Ivan Illich brilliantly exposed them, offering a surprising diagnosis with a level of ethical reflection rarely heard of again.

Wolfgang Sachs, Wuppertal Institute, Berlin
Planet Dialectics: Explorations in Environment & Development

Stop trying to grow the economy and green up energy consumption! Try, instead, to figure out how best to live. Sajay Samuel's new collection of essays by Ivan Illich inspires us all to hope for and work on radically discovering the kinds of lives that we have forgotten that we know how to live.

William Ray Arney, Evergreen State College
Educating for Freedom

After reading Illich one learns to see the world anew. Environmentalists and scholars are guided through the dangers and limitations of both economic and ecological constructs in this collection of essays. After reading them one is opened up to new possibilities for both thought and action.

Dean Bavington, Memorial University
Managed Annihilation: An unnatural history of the Newfoundland Cod Collapse

In the 1970s Illich's explorations of an alternative to the modern economic infatuation with scarcity and the hubris of ecological responsibility seemed to many like wild, eccentric provocations. Now a decade after Illich's death, this modest volume attempts to recover and re-introduce in a new century insights that have only grown more pertinent.

Carl Mitcham, Colorado School of Mines
Thinking through Technology

Even if written in the 1970s, these essays of Ivan Illich have lost none of their pertinence or newness. They help us sidestep the heedless rush towards catastrophe brought on by an out-of-control techno-economic mega-machine.

Serge Latouche, Emeritus, University Paris-Sud
Farewell to Growth